HOW GET OUT

OF AN

ABUSIVE RELATIONSHIP

(WITH YOURSELF)

CAREY WILKINSON LEE

Copyright © 2020 Carey Wilkinson Lee

Layout by Lyndsie Barrie and Carey Wilkinson Lee
Cover design by Lyndsie Barrie
Cover photography by Joanne Howard

Request permission to reproduce parts of this publication, other than brief quotations, at careywilkinsonlee.com/contact.

Thank You

Thank YOU for reading my words. And to all of the amazing people who boosted my confidence by preordering the book.

This book would 100% not exist without some serious time commitment, brave contributions, unwavering support and a humbling respect for the author. These incredibly FABulous women have me struggling for words to write, from places in my heart I didn't know existed until now.

THANK YOU Lyndsie Barrie, Laurey Godard, Ashley Fox, Jean Wilkinson, Sharon Wilkinson, Ute Gilbert, Laurie Lakeman, Tracy Guthrie, Camryn Guthrie, Joanne Howard, Andrea Carlson, Marcela Montes-Lobos, Alannah Jensen, Stef Scottaline, Sandy Maloy, Melissa Pearce and Michelle Fleischhacher.

THANK YOU Mom and Dad for our endless, enlightening conversations, the safe and loving doors that are always open and the countless, exceptional life opportunities. Jesse, for your insight, patience and wit. Truly you are my very favourite human. I didn't write anything embarrassing …I don't think - better read the book. Derek, for your ENDLESS patience, commitment to understand and unwavering devotion.
I Love you. Xox

Contents

Once Upon a Time...

One sunny Saturday morning in the Spring of 1996, I went for a walk. I was walking alone down Stephen Avenue in Calgary close to the bachelor apartment I was renting. After moving from my born-and-raised town of Edmonton, I was truly independent for the first time in my life. I had graduated from my second college program that spring, had a super cute, ideally located apartment and an awesome paying, full-time job in marketing. Everyone I loved was healthy and I had some solid, happy and supportive friends.

That day, I knew I looked good. I'm not really one to invest too much time in primping, but I remember that I invested a bit of extra time in my physical appearance on this particular day. Unfortunately, looking good didn't equal feeling good. Ironically, extra efforts in my appearance usually brought on extra scrutiny. When I put on mascara, I felt more insecure than without it.

I had a whole day of freedom in front of me to discover the treasures of my new Calgary neighbourhood! Really, there was nothing negative I could draw on to justify my negative mindset. It was a perfect fall day and even though I put in the extra effort to look good, I felt exposed and vulnerable - like a fake. I really just wanted to buy some comfort snacks, walk back home, put on pjs and watch a movie. I knew I was fragile and vulnerable emotionally, but I was determined to do something with my day. Mostly, it was so I could say (to whom I'm not sure), that I had had the best day ever! (If social media had been part of my life back then, my anxiety would have been tripled!) I also knew very well the guilt I would feel if I wasted a beautiful sunny day full of potential outstanding adventures. Truth be told, it didn't matter how I spent my time that day, it would never be good enough. The pressure I put on myself to live the perfect day was suffocating and unrealistic.

I don't remember having expectations, but I definitely did not expect the street to be so full of people when I ventured out that day. I've never considered myself claustrophobic, but I found I couldn't take 3 steps without brushing up against someone else and I didn't like it.

With every single person I saw, I passed a judgement on myself. It was fast and furious and I could actually physically FEEL the judgement. If you are someone who has never been in a situation like this, it might be hard to understand. Those of you that are picking up exactly what I am putting down - it's a really scary place to be. Each thought and observation was like a physical shot in the gut. I was mentally in a fist fight with myself and was getting brutally hit from all sides. It's impossible to know now if I was making it all up, getting a sixth sense, picking up on others' energies or reading non-verbal cues. It really doesn't matter the root of it, the blows felt abusive, unfair and left me feeling raw and frazzled.

A visual from the Alice in Wonderland movie comes to mind. There is a scene from the cartoon, when Alice drinks from the little "drink me" bottle and she shrinks into a tiny version of herself. Alice is caught unaware, her body is unfamiliar to her and she doesn't have control over what is happening. For my particular scenario, add thousands of persistent, unrelenting, tiny bees with their goal to sting. With each stranger, (without a clue if any of these people were ones I would admire or would even want to consider their opinion) I was absorbing negative judgement and I was shrinking into a tiny, weak, invisible, battered version of myself.

To add to my discomfort, anxiety and the weight of my self loathing, I was hyper aware, and completely confident every other person on that street was happy, successful, content and living their best life. Every stranger, in my mind, was living a better life than me, happier than me, more worthy than me. My expectations and pressure for the perfect day, combined with self-judgement and insecurities, became too much for me to handle that day.

I was fully aware that I SHOULD be a carefree, independent young woman, but I simply, at that moment, had the feeling that I was disappearing. Like a beautiful, fluffy, pink, sweet bundle of cotton candy caught in the rain. I was quickly and completely disintegrating.

All of this was 100% self-inflicted and the creative work of my brain.

I don't remember much after that, but I did make it home and lived to tell this (very non-Disney) tale. I knew then it was time for me to get help. Fabulous Alice found a way out and eventually I did, too. But it sure was, and still can be, a struggle.

Since the defining moment on Stephen Avenue, I've had many therapist visits, surrounded myself with fabulous people, made my family a priority, became more consistent with doctor visits, tried alternative remedies (Reiki, St. John's Wart), made sleep and exercise a priority and I even joined a bowling league!

The abuse was real and toxic and I seriously started to not like myself. I knew I was being self-centered and if I was going to make a positive impact on this world, I needed to get serious about ending this unsupportive relationship.

Despite being completely confused and overwhelmed, I made the conscious decision to NOT FOCUS on the WHY. Instead, I decided to identify the abusive behaviours, find solutions and start rewiring my brain. That intensive process lead me to writing this book.

My brain had the power to create all of the chaos so I knew it could also create a beautiful, calm and inspiring place. Becoming aware, consistently stopping ugly, mean thoughts and trusting myself has rewired my brain. I now have the power to create the life I want. From medications and therapy, to dancing and crying, to chakra clearing and intense, honest conversations, the mission was to become my own best friend. To treat myself with respect, kindness and understanding.

"Nothing in the world is worth having or worth doing unless it means effort, pain, difficulty... I have never in my life envied a human being who led an easy life. I have envied a great many people who led difficult lives and led them well."

- Theodore Roosevelt

To make this book a simple, impactful read, I took all of the learning, practices, struggles and tricks and sorted them into 3 categories:

1. The Secret to Life (wait for it!)

2. Trust

3. Be in The Moment

The goal of sharing my journey is to reach those who struggle with low self-esteem and negative self-talk. The solutions that helped me rewire my brain fill these pages, but it isn't a quick fix - I still work at it everyday. But I have learned that if you commit to patience, awareness, consistency and to Love* yourself, life can become magical.

*The word "Love" is always capitalized in this book. To me, Love is trust, kindness and respect and it deserves a capital L.

Compiled in these pages are 21 (and 4 bonus) of the most effective tricks I've used in the last 30 years to rewire my brain. I have found them magical which is what the wand logo symbolizes. I recommend that you pick 1 or 2 to start, commit to practicing them for a minimum of 21 days, then incorporate more. They have been strategically placed throughout the book and can be found at the back for quick reference. I use a variation of several daily.

You'll know you're at the end of a FAB Mind Trick when you see this:

1. The Relationship

"You're entirely bonkers.
But I'll tell you a secret. All the best people are."

- Alice in Wonderland

Recently I realized (with a BIG burst of magical clarity), my low self esteem had me trapped in an abusive relationship with myself. After 30+ years of struggling and searching and bumbling about, I felt the relief of awareness, but also super afraid of the work ahead. What now? Where do I start? I couldn't just pack up the car and drive away from my own brain! I couldn't escape by ending a relationship, moving away, changing my name or getting a restraining order. Often I felt there was no escape.

My abuser, like many abusers, slowly eroded my confidence over time. It had me feeling worthless and powerless.

Once I started trusting and sharing my crazy thoughts with others, it surprised a lot of people in my life. Many were shocked at the private anguish I put myself through. I am a social person, I had a very safe and privileged childhood and I was very good at presenting as happy and positive. There is a huge difference between being "quiet" and being "calm". I became good at having an "outside" face, which was on when I was around other people and an "inside" face that only I saw. I was fully aware that no one knew the real me. I knew she was there but she was locked away. I couldn't get to her.

I constantly felt like a HUGE mess. I truly **didn't know who I was**, what I wanted or where I fit into this world. Nothing I did was ever enough or productive enough. Nothing I accomplished in my day felt like enough. I thought I needed to have THE "right" answer to questions about my life, hobbies, family and career. My autopilot ran from a place where the mission was to be liked/loved, admired even. But not because of who I am at the core. I didn't know who that woman was. I remember wanting to be athletic but in reality, I am a reader. I Love to watch sports but don't really like to play them. I played soccer for a few years and it completely stressed me out. It made me realize that I hate to be chased!

"Who in the world am I? Ah, that's the great puzzle!"
- Alice in Wonderland

My thoughts generally had a negative voice and insisted I worry about events happening two weeks in the future or ones from the past. I would listen to the negative voices, believe them and I usually didn't question if they were valid or not.

I found I became emotionally overwhelmed easily and daily by things I couldn't control. Things like recycling. I would go through the act of recycling 100% of everything I could, but then I would be worried about what happened after I washed and sorted and took it to the depot. I was diligent, but was it really making a difference?

The crazy part was that at some level I knew I was abusing myself, but I didn't know how to stop. It was EXHAUSTING. I

knew my own thoughts were keeping me from living a fulfilling life but I was too overwhelmed and exhausted to try and fix it.

Descriptive scenarios have helped me communicate what is happening in my head. They force me to really dig deep and create relatable situations. Strong visuals have been helpful to share with others who want to understand, but have never experienced mental health struggles. This visual lead to the title of this book:

I'm running in pitch black woods and, while I'm trying to run, (from what, I'm not sure… anxiety?) I just keep stumbling over roots, rocks and brush. It's raining a heavy, consistent mist and the wind is relentless, coming from all directions. My hair is whipping in my face. I keep plunging blindly forward, full of cuts and bruises. The intensity to finally arrive at a place where I can feel safe, peaceful, loved is desperate, but I don't know where it is or even if I'm heading in the right direction. I'm broken and crying, but I don't give up or stop. I keep fighting to get there, but who I'm fighting, I have no idea.

That crazy scenario was a common place for my mind to be. It was ugly, confusing and disastrous at times. Over the years I have been tested and questioned by professionals and was eventually diagnosed with anxiety, although I've never experienced a full-blown panic attack. Existing with a brain like mine, it was easy to self medicate (read more about self medicating with alcohol on page 96) with patio drinks and make uninformed, impulsive decisions. Some days I felt very immature indeed. These episodes are rare now, but it took years of searching, crying, suffering, frustration and self loathing.

I was surprised to learn that research estimates humans have about 40,000-70,000 thoughts every day. I am VERY sure that I break the ceiling of this statistic daily. I now credit this to my brilliant, multi-tasking, yet to be understood or diagnosed ADD (attention deficit disorder) brain. It was an out of control superpower, which is the topic of my second book (coming in 2021).

It has been an exhausting journey, but I've trained my brain to be kind, patient, feel worthy, trust and let go of past hurts and disappointments that don't serve me anymore. To focus on the potential in myself and embrace life as an awesome adventure.

2. The Secret To Life

Finding the secret to a content life became my mission. I knew that once I found it, I would live by it to help me navigate life in a positive way. I finally found it in my early forties.

One night when I was 16, I was home alone watching a movie. I was wrapped up all cozy on the couch, eating popcorn (which was a staple in our house), watching the movie "City Slickers" with Billy Crystal (Mitch) & Jack Palance (Earl).

I was loving the movie and near the end, a scene came up that made my whole body sit up and pay attention. With my eyes intent on the screen and my hearing dial turned up to maximum, I was full of anticipation. The characters on the screen had my full attention. Curly was about to tell Mitch…

I Found It!

In mere seconds, all was going to be revealed to me and I was ready grab a hold of it!

Mitch was struggling to figure out what the meaning of life was and Curly, who was wise and respected had the answer. This is what they said:

Curly : Do you know what the secret of life is?
[holds up one finger]
Curly : This.
Mitch : Your finger?
Curly : One thing. Just one thing. You stick to that and the rest don't mean shit.
Mitch : But, what is the "one thing?"
And then Curly (with his damn finger still in the air) says:
Curly : *[smiles]* That's what YOU have to find out.

Like, WHAT??? I was so mad! A second before, I was on top of the world and the next I was tumbling down, and it was now out of my grasp. The contrast of emotions was overwhelming. It took me a minute to recover and then I ejected the damn VHS and threw it on the floor. Take that Curly, you ass*%^&!

Immediately after my outburst, the question flashed like a large neon sign in my head. It was branded into my brain: WHAT IS THE SECRET TO LIFE? What is the one thing? As far fetched as it seemed, I knew in my gut that there was a simple, manageable secret to life. Despite the many factors that contribute to good living, they all hinge on a central, critical factor: The One Thing.

Finding the key that Curly smugly kept to himself became an obsession. Now that I have my answer, how perfect and simple it is, I can't believe it took me so long to find it. Subconsciously I think I have known it for years, even before the "City Slickers" tape met its tragic end. One word. Simple and beautiful.

  Like a gift I'd earned for the time I've spent on this planet dedicated to the task, it appeared in my head, and I left like Indiana Jones after finding the arc. I had discovered a treasure.

The power of the discovery rocked me to my core and set me on a beautiful path with the secret that is always tucked in my pocket is…

Artist - Camryn Guthrie

KINDNESS.

The One Thing. Simple and free. And reaps endless rewards.

Kindness has become my religion. It is the seed, soil, sunlight, water, fertilizer, Love, nurturing - everything required to build a beautiful, strong, healthy life. For both the receiver of the kindness and for the one giving it. Kindness. Being kind and making someone else feel cared for or make them smile (at the very least) feels fantastic. I believe offering and receiving kindness in everything you do is a life-changing practice that ensures fulfillment, contentment, purposeful days and peaceful nights. In my opinion, kindness is the secret to a good life!

Imagine (John Lennon did) a world in which we are ALL kind to one another. A world where disdain for differences doesn't exist. Instead, we celebrate our individuality while recognizing our shared experience of being on this earth.

I believe our bodies, at their cellular and most sub-conscious levels, recognize kindness as a form of healing and respond by releasing healing energy. I have felt the change - beautiful and instant. The thing I find so cool about kindness is that we never really know the impressive impact it has on ourselves and others. Kindness gives us magical powers to create a ridiculously safe, compassionate, yet adventurous and fulfilling world.

**Now I find simply being kind
to everyone is enough. That is the goal of my day.**

When kindness began to be a prominent focus in my life, I slept better, laughed harder and began trusting myself and others to be genuine. Being kind in every interaction, no matter how minor, doesn't take any more time than actions dominated by mean-spiritedness or ambivalence. Even if we are feeling angry and impatient, we can still be kind. I believe wholeheartedly kindness is the best investment you can make in life. The benefits are overwhelming and limitless.

Awareness

*"Awareness is a key ingredient in success.
If you have it, teach it, if you lack it, seek it."*

- Michael B. Kitson, Historian

The first step for me in healing from anything in my life is awareness. It starts with becoming aware of how I am contributing to standing in my own way. I identify thoughts and habits and prioritize them:

1. What is the actual problem?
2. Trust I will find a solution.
3. What help do I need?

I found the magic in awareness was that solutions started presenting themselves when I was least expecting them. Once aware of the problem, the intention was set to find a solution. I discovered that if I let it all percolate for a while, answers would come while my mind was busy doing other things. Often they would be random, instant and unexpected, but a completely clear solution would present itself.

There are so many amazing people who dedicate their lives to helping others heal. Once aware of the problem, there is someone with a specific skillset to help. Just a few options are: medical doctor, naturopathic practitioners, chiropractors, massage therapists, personal trainers, nutritionists, psychologists, therapists, dentists, life coaches and mentors, energy work healers (balance chakras and/or ego) and alternative therapies. I also benefitted greatly from and loved EFT (emotional freedom technique) & CBT (cognitive behaviour therapy).

AWARENESS is the key, Baby!

#1. Negative to Positive

This mind trick was LIFE-CHANGING! Bringing awareness to and catching all of the negative narrative without a judgemental eye, gave me a running start to healing. It had such a positive impact and gave me the confidence I needed to know I was going to be free of my abusive thoughts.

This FAB Trick takes a commitment and can be intense but I found once the thoughts started to flow, it was easy. Find a journal and carry it with you everywhere you go. Write down and record every SINGLE negative thought that comes to your mind. EVERY negative thought or word. Take it with you in the car (pull over to write), into stores, to the bathroom. Have it with you while exercising, while you cook, in bed. I suggest having it with you always. If you forget the journal, leave a voice message for yourself and then write down your thoughts as soon as you can. Get every poisonous thought, voice and word out! Be curious and observe what comes up. Don't over think them or make any judgements.

Catching them all took awhile but the 2nd part of the process is a lot faster. For each negative, write a positive to replace it. This was so important for me because when one of the pesky buggers would show up, it was easy to stop and replace it with something kind and supportive. This is HUGE. It is a mind trick that I have done a few times and will always be in my tool kit.

Negatives	Positives
I have no self confidence	I walk tall, proud & confident
I've wasted too much time	Everything I have done has a purpose
I am not a good parent	I know how to be a good parent
I should be more adventurous	I try new things
All I ever do is worry	I let go of things I can't control
I should exercise more	I get my body moving so it is healthy
I aways say the wrong thing	I think before I speak. It is ok to say the wrong thing

To make it easy, on the following pages there is room for you to write your negative and positive thoughts.

Negatives   Positives

_____   _____

_____   _____

_____   _____

_____   _____

Negatives

Positives

Negatives

_____

_____

_____

_____

_____

_____

_____

_____

_____

_____

_____

_____

_____

_____

_____

Positives

_____

_____

_____

_____

_____

_____

_____

_____

_____

_____

_____

_____

_____

_____

_____

The first time I did this, it took about a week to feel that I had captured it all. I was shocked to see how many negative,

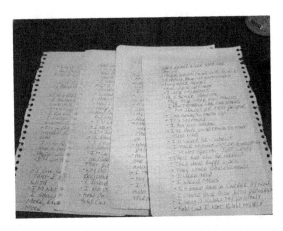

unsupportive thoughts casually sauntered through my brain every day. I had pages and pages and pages.

This is why I think literally writing down the thoughts in one place is important.

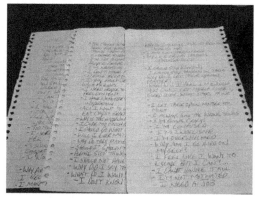

They don't seem as harmful on their own, but seeing them all together shocked me enough to evoke a desperate need for change. I would never have said the words I was writing down to someone I cared about but I was poisoning myself with them aggressively. This exercise was intrusive to my day at first, but it became a revelation and a source of power to see them all exposed and written down in front of me.

A visual I use to describe how effective the Negative to Positive was to clear my brain is catching a bunch of teenagers, in my house, having a house party. I visualize coming home, opening the door, and when I turn the lights on, my house is full of young partiers! Some see me right away and run. It takes others a bit longer. Some smile and casually make their way out. A few ask if they can just stay for a few more drinks. It takes a while, but eventually I get them all out. Some do come back for a visit. I might even let them stay for a while, but my house isn't full of unwanted guests anymore. I found that once I caught them in the act, became aware that they are abusive (and more importantly, not true!) they didn't have any power over my self esteem. And if they did show up, I would give them a smile, thank them for coming, tell them now is not a good time and close the door.

So now what? Every time a negative makes an appearance, use FAB Trick #2 as soon as you become aware of it...

Fab Mind Trick

#2. Stop.

Just STOP. Catch the thought as soon as you become aware of it. Visualizing a huge stop sign works for me. Stop the thought, take 3 super huge deep breaths and then tell yourself something positive. If you are remembering a moment in the past that you are reliving and feeling regret about, STOP, breath and say something like, "I am doing the best I can. I am learning and making informed choices." I still depend on this trick daily, but

I am catching the thoughts way faster - before they have a chance to affect my physical and mental space is my goal.

Fab Mind Trick

#3. Do. Don't Think.

Start doing something - anything to distract you.

- Colour, draw, write, do push ups, call a friend, write a letter.
- Focus on getting ready and go for a walk (FAB Trick #15. Feel, See, Hear to get grounded), take some pictures. Look for the ordinary miracles that surround you.
- Make dinner, sing, dance, play with the dog/kids, organize the basement or garage. Do a Negative to Positive list!

Take a shower. When I'm feeling overwhelmed and about to snap, a shower is calming and gives my mind something else to focus on. Showers also stimulate our senses (feel, see, hear, smell) which always helps me feel grounded.

I categorized all of my negative thoughts to see if an identifiable, workable problem became obvious. I wanted a word, a target that I could focus my efforts on. I went through my list and found they fit into 5 major categories:

- Ego
- Empathy
- Comparison
- Judgement
- Jealously

As with FAB Mind Tricks, I decided to focus on just one of these at a time. I am a huge fan of the 21-Day Meditation Experiences[1] by Deepak Chopra and Oprah Winfrey. This is how 21 became my number. Focusing on one or two for 21 days keeps it simple. Be like an eagle who is laser focused on its prey. This gave me something to work on everyday but simplified the task. Patience is your friend during these days. It can be a long but beautiful journey.

Ego

> *"The Ego, however, is not who you really are.*
> *The ego is your self-image; it is your social mask;*
> *it is the role you are playing. Your social mask thrives on approval. It wants control, and it is sustained by power, because it lives in fear."*
>
> *- Deepak Chopra*

I realized that my ego could be the culprit for causing me to overthink and creating scenarios that were making me feel panic, rushed and overwhelmed. I learned that all humans have an ego, and it has a huge impact on how we treat ourselves. The ego doesn't live in the now, but always in fear. It never makes you feel equal, but always that you are better (high ego) or worse (low ego) than others.

---

[1] chopracentermeditation.com

**Ego always makes you feel better or worse.
Never equal to others.**

The low ego is where I was functioning from. That big long list of negatives I wrote down in my negative/positive journal proved to me how strong my low ego was.

Worrying about what others think was my ego worrying that it/ we were going to be left out. Just becoming aware that my low ego was contributing to so many negative thoughts helped me to start healing. Paying attention to my ego and get to know it became my 1st 21 day priority. When I started to talk to my ego and smother it with Love and kindness, I saw it as a scared little child instead of a powerful force.

"It's none of my business what you think of me."
- *Peter Baksa*

Peter Baksa's book, 'It's None of my Business what you Think of me." came into my life at the exact time that I needed it. I believe most books that are given to us or catch our attention do. Peter thinks that "The most expensive liability we have in our possession is our ego." It's our ego that seeks other people's approval.

I started doing a very simple exercise to balance my ego. The goal in balancing my ego was to be functioning from my higher self (coming from my higher self means living from a place of kindness, gratitude, trust and no judgement). To feel equal and not feel as though I am lesser or greater than anyone else or that anyone else is greater or lesser than me.

Fab Mind Trick

#4. Balance Your Ego.

When I started, I balanced my ego two times a day, once in the morning and once at night. I found that the effects were almost instant. When functioning from my higher self, my emotions don't affect me physically. My mind is more decisive and I am able to listen to and trust my instincts.

I have been balancing my ego everyday for over 10 years. It's very little effort for a huge result (in my opinion). It can be done anytime, anywhere, several times a day.

- Take 3 deep breaths.

- Say in your head or out loud "Today I come from my higher self and I balance my ego."

- Repeat at least 7 times. I keep saying it until I feel that my body is responding to the message (I feel a shift in my consciousness and awareness). The goal is to be balanced and make decisions today from that place.

- End with "This is my truth."

I still balance my ego daily. It amazes me how life-changing a 30 second mind trick can be.

Note: Balancing the ego was introduced to me by Canadian visionary, published author, internationally renowned intuitive counsellor and spiritual mentor (for adults and teenagers) Tara Taylor.[2]

Don't Take Things Personally

"Do not take things personally. Period."

- Peter Baksa

Is that even possible? I instantly loved this idea but I was not convinced I would ever pull it off. The concept was also introduced to me in Peter's Book.

When I read "Do not take things personally. Period." It gave me a very exciting and lofty goal.

On page 116, he writes: "When you take something personally, the word is speaking to your ego that grows and acts in response." When we are young, "we learn to take everything personally. We are taught that the world revolves around us and that if we act in a certain way, we can achieve what we desire."

"But the fact is," this is a sentence that caused a HUGE shift for me, "nothing others do is related to you; what they do is because of their own selves. Each of us live in our own dream of existence in our own mind. Others are in a completely different world than the one we live in."

He explains, "The opinions that others say and do are in accordance to their conditioning. Their point of view and perspective is an outcropping of a belief system, set of memes,

---

[2] tarataylor.com

contracts and agreements they have learned. Someone might object to your appearance, actions, way of living, but it always relates to something this person is dealing with in their own world."

**"When you take it personally, you become fair game.
It makes you easy prey."**

I became aware of the concept and noticed when I was taking things personally. I found it a very fascinating subject and started to research it more. For me, a main contributor to stop taking things personally was understanding perspective.

Perception and Perspective

*"Sometimes it's a good idea to turn the couch around.
Check out the view from the other direction."*

- Me

These two are an interesting, complex pair!

Perception is what we interpret. Our understanding and meaning of a given situation or person/s. Perceptions are typically developed from our beliefs which are developed over time or sometimes from a life-changing event. When we have beliefs about something, those beliefs factor into how we perceive meaning from any situation.

Perspective is our point of view. It's the lens that we see the world through. It determines how we view ourselves, others and everything around us. "Keep things in perspective" means to look at the picture as a whole, to take a step back and see things in their proper relation to everything else, to logically take a look at a situation and assess it (hopefully) before we react.

The mind-blowing part for me was that our perspectives and perceptions can be based on so many factors beyond our control.[3] Many of them we might not even be aware of:

- Beliefs we are raised with
- Our values
- What you can see or can't
- What you think you know or don't know
- Past social situations
- Your current state of physical health
- World issues affecting you
- What you hear or actually don't hear
- Where your mind is at the time (what is going on in your life and in that immediate moment)
- Expectations

I think it's almost impossible to try and grasp how humongous our perception and perspective affect every interaction in our lives. We all have years and generations of thoughts, opinions, experiences. Some come from sources seen and some unseen. We develop our own perception/perspective and it is mixed with others from almost everyone who has come into our lives.

After learning a little bit about perception and perspective, I found it easier to let go of feeling judgement from others and not take things personally.

---

[3] pediaa.com (2017) Difference Between Perception and Perspective. Https://pediaa.com/difference-between-perception-and-perspective/

Fab Mind Trick

#5. Positive Affirmations.

Any Saturday Night Live fans in the house? The Stuart Smalley skits and his daily affirmations were one of my favourites. They made me laugh but also introduced me to the power of positive affirmations. Ironic and fabulous that SNL gave me this one. I have used them consistently when the negative brain tries to over power the positive.

Works best if done at least once daily. But not limited to just once.

Take 3 deep breaths and read your Positive Affirmations out loud:

Today I trust that I am exactly where I am meant to be. Don't forget the infinite possibilities that you were born with. I wish you contentment with who you are and that you use and share your unique gifts in this world.

- To get more Love, I simply have to Love myself more
- I allow myself to think big dreams
- I attract only good things in my life
- I am unique with my own path to follow

- I am courageous and brave
- I like the way I look
- I am powerful
- I am a good sleeper
- I am beautiful inside and out
- I am safe. In my house, in my town, in my world
- I am a fast learner
- I have lots of great ideas. I am very creative
- I am a good influence on others
- I deserve good things
- I recognize all of the gifts in my life. I focus on the positive
- I can do anything I set my mind to. My dreams are coming true

Customize your Positive Affirmations list, print it and put where you can see it daily. Make more than 1 if you want.

An Empath in this (crazy) World

"Empathy is really the opposite of spiritual meanness.
It's the capacity to understand that every war is both won and lost. And that someone else's pain is as meaningful as your own."

- Barbara Kingsolver

Being an extremely empathetic person was a major contributor to my abusive relationship. I wouldn't (or couldn't) let myself be happy when there can be much human and animal suffering on our earth. Navigating a content, fulfilling life in a sometimes (often) superficial, war torn, Hollywood, greedy, GMO filled, profit driven, social media obsessed, unpredictable world, where lots of people don't even have their basic needs met, can be

VERY difficult for an empathetic person. I've worked to make empathy a gift instead of a curse. The curse always seemed to be the dominant force. It had me leaving movies (Blood Diamond) because I was crying so hard, walking the neighbourhood to save as many earthworms as possible after a rainstorm (could I have saved more?) and almost having a panic attack in Walmart imagining where all the bloody packaging was going to end up!

Where there is pain and hurt, I feel desperate to help. I put myself in the shoes of those suffering and it can take me deep to a place where I can actually feel others' emotions, confusion, pain, frustration, desperation and heartache. Just to name a few. I really wish I didn't do this to myself. It happens so fast sometimes, that if I let my guard down, it can ruin my day in 10 seconds or less.

The way my empathetic brain operated on autopilot was EXHAUSTING. I would just let my mind saunter into situations and allow it to take me wherever it wished. It felt as though it was taking my hand, my most trusted and loved friend, and guiding me with a smile saying "Don't be scared. Don't worry. You are safe with me." But I wasn't! I would follow along and walk right into some of the most horrific scenarios.

During the 2020 pandemic, I was lounging on my bed with my pup, Bella. I was thinking about how we are struggling as a world right now and comparing it to times in the past. As a historical fiction reader, I have been introduced to many different stories from around the world. I let my mind drift and before I knew what was happening, I was under the floor of a farmhouse during the Holocaust. A beautiful, dirty and scared little girl was hiding there, all alone. I let myself imagine exactly how that would feel. To be hungry, cold and ragged but also to have no idea of your fate. Would they find you today? Would they kill you instantly as well as the owners of the house? Did she see her family get killed or taken away? Were they alive, captured or hiding too? THEN I imagined how she would feel if she was caught. Listening to the boots upstairs and knowing she was about to be discovered. It feels like I'm temporarily in a trance when I let my brain take me on an empathy journey. I am almost paralyzed in that moment. Most of the time, I have to physically shake myself out of it.

When I think of the suffering of children or animals, I feel a physical ache. I feel deeply about our earth as well; all the waste that is causing damage and hurting those that inhabit it. I physically ache and often cry for women who have been or are being abused. Parents who have lost a child. Parents who have children but feel trapped and scared for their future. The victims of a drunk driving accident, but also the one who caused the crash and each person in their families.

If you are also an empath, you understand. The consistent practice of bringing myself into the present moment (see page 93) has been ridiculously helpful. And finding ways to help others in my community (see page 101) as close to the front lines as possible, has helped alleviate the pressure to cure the entire world. Be kind, serve, help, smile and give someone else a reason to smile.

Fab Mind Trick

#6. Don't Watch the News.

When we would watch the evening news, my dad would tell me, "If it doesn't bleed, it doesn't lead." This meant that the news usually focuses on "bleed" or shocking, terrible stories. For an empath, this can have an instant, negative effect (especially at night before bed). I also stay away from shows and movies about abuse, abductions, killers, cruelty to animals. I'm not saying to not be aware of how we can make our world a better place. But hearing and seeing stories about evil and we can't do anything to change or stop it can be extremely overwhelming.

#7. Talk to Your Angels.

I believe in angels. I believe that we are born with them around us. They stay close and are there waiting for the second we need them. When I am feeling lost, scared, worried about my family or the future or at a point where I am feeling helpless, I talk to them. First, I always thank them for everything they do that I don't see. Then I wish, tell, ask, cry and pray. I can feel that I am being heard. My body shifts to a place of peace and relief and I feel, without a doubt, that I am not alone. We are never alone. Our angels are guarding over us, instantly ready to help.

Comparison

"All of you people, in a big world out there,
find out who you are and try not to be afraid of it."
- Drew Barrymore (movie Never Been Kissed)

I was always, ALWAYS comparing myself to others. It was ridiculous, non stop and it is seriously unquantifiable! Comparison was an obvious contributing factor (to my dis-ease) but when it literally jumped out at me from my computer screen, I knew I needed to pay more attention.

Has a quote or phrase ever just popped up right in front of you that felt like it was meant for you to see? Something your intuition screams at you to pay attention to?

Note: I know my instincts are guiding me when I feel a physical knot in my stomach and a goose bump feeling goes through my whole body. I also get an overwhelming feeling of knowing. Knowing that this is something that deserves my attention. How we trust and understand what our instincts are trying to say is different for all of us. If you are not sure how your instincts? See Footnote.[4]

This is that paragraph that jumped out at me:

> **"Comparison is a killer. Cut it out!**
>
> **From the shape of our cells to the swirl of our fingerprints, each human is profoundly, almost incomprehensibly unique. In the eons of time, amongst trillions of human eggs that have been fertilized and hatched there is only one you. Microscopically remarkable, positively unrepeatable, original and BEYOND COMPARE."**
>
> **- Unknown**

[4]thelawofattraction.com/learn-trust-intuition/

After reading it through a few times, I knew instantly that comparison was something I was doing consistently and relentlessly. Realizing the power of this new treasure, I printed the page, cut it out (so I don't have a source), and put it on my bedside table. I started using it as a bookmark to keep the message accessible and so that it would sink in daily.

One simple, 10 letter word had been causing me a lot of grief: comparison. FINALLY I caught one of the annoying culprits and now, because I was aware of it, I would be able to stop it from doing any more damage.

So, what to do with an habitual behaviour that you have just become aware of? I decided that the first thing I had to do was START to STOP. I had to make a conscious effort to start stopping comparing myself, choices, family, past, hair colour/length, cooking abilities, fashion choices ... everything really, to others.

It wasn't easy to rewire my brain to stop comparing, but the more I was aware of it and stopped it from happening, the easier it got.

Do you compare your life, habits, Sunday rituals, holidays, jobs, cars ... (the list is endless) to others? If you are a victim of comparisons and you are now aware you are doing it, WHOOOHOOO! This is a major, fantastic first step.

From the positive side of the Negative vs Positive exercise on Page 23, I found it helpful to write down and display the positive statements on sticky notes beside my bed to read each night. I need to be ready to replace unwanted, self-defeating negative comparisons with uplifting, positive thoughts and feelings.

#8. Zip Yourself Up.

This beauty goes way back for me. I found it worked instantly and I Love it because it lets me stay in bed a bit longer. I did it every morning for months and I pull it out when lacking confidence or inspiration.

Essentially, this is a "fake it until you make it" exercise. It is a visualization that has you zipping yourself up in a whole new body. The body of the person you want to be. It helped me to get into a mental state where I felt like I could conquer the day ahead.

- Start at your toes. What do they look like? Mine are always super cute. My feet? Like I just had a pedicure yesterday.
- I make myself a little taller - my legs are longer (as well as hairless and completely smooth).
- In my zip up visualization, I don't have any knee pain and I am dressed in a comfy yet very stylish outfit.

Move up your entire body, visualizing how you want to feel and present yourself to the world that day. For me, I am feeling decisive, adventurous and excited to find out what the day ahead of me has to offer. My zipped up version of myself is a confident, competent mom who is grateful for the little things and recognizes the gifts that life has to offer. She is laughing, has a quick wit and is mentally prepared for the battle of another day.

Zip yourself up every morning. And in between if you want to.

Judgement

"God forbid you ever had to walk a mile in their shoes. Then you really might know what it's like."

- Song 'What it's like' by Everest

A definition of judgement: The ability to make considered decisions or come to sensible conclusions.

For me, judgement was similar to comparison but ran deeper. Self judgement had the power to derail fun, dreams and genuine connections. Judgement was a huge obstacle for me even to write these very words you are reading right now (so awesome, thank you!). How could I write a book to help others? My problems aren't really problems. The ones I have are such first world issues. I'll be perceived as weak, ungrateful, a complainer. How could my annoying, self-centred mental health issues possibly help someone else? What experience or struggles have I had to endure to justify me writing (and others actually wanting to read) a whole book?

That judgemental voice had me stuck. I had a vision of myself chained to a post. I'm in a beautiful farm meadow. I am surrounded by rolling fields scattered with flowers of all sorts and colours. The green and lush land is full of perfectly placed and full trees and it stretches as far as my eye can see. I'm healthy, calm and capable. I'm wearing a vintage sundress and my hair flows long, blond and the perfect beach messy but sexy. I am surrounded by beauty and potential. All I have to do is decide to walk away.

BUT, the huge, thick chain of judgement/self doubt had a firm hold. Self-judgement became even more significant when I became a parent. However awesome and super cute and loved (and did I say AWESOME!) my baby boy was, becoming a parent WHOOSHed my insecurities to the surface. To make a long story short:

- I was a new mom
- Had been given a mild postpartum diagnosis
- Was working 4 days a week
- One day I started fainting downtown at a work lunch
- A simple surgery to fix an ectopic rupture, turned into major surgery

While The 2004 Calgary Stampede celebrated around me, I found myself:

- Unemployed
- Unqualified to claim Employment Insurance
- Sad, weak, bruised
- Was told future pregnancies unlikely
- Home alone to perseverate on anything I may have done to cause this

I felt that my body had betrayed me and a lot of pride and worth can be associated with being fertile. Back in the day, women would be beheaded if they couldn't get pregnant. Would I be able to let myself feel like a successful woman if I couldn't get pregnant again?

Now a stay-at-home mom, I had been unable to recover my pride, worth or understand what my instincts were trying to tell me. I knew how lucky I was to have my perfect son and I was

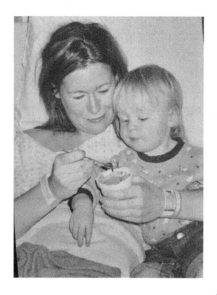

desperate to just feel grateful. I was searching for purpose and constantly judged my decisions as a parent. The mix (as well as eventually going on fertility drugs) was that I was in a constant and perpetual state of feeling overwhelmed. My mind raced and stressed over simple things like meal planning and providing the healthiest snacks, our recycling system, running water, leaving the fridge door open, to larger issues like loved ones dying, my health, humans (and animals) in our world who are scared, sad, alone, sick. And, still all the while, I was trying to present myself as perfect - happy, totally chill, capable and trusting that my dream career would be waiting for me. AND not asking for help. I wanted to just be grateful to be alive. In hindsight, it probably wasn't the best idea to go on fertility drugs, but alas.

Note: I used EAB Mind Trick #8 - Zip Yourself Up - a lot during this time.

The invention of the internet didn't help. Having 24/7 access to others' highlight reels, my perceived short-comings would scream at me in all corners at all times.

Judgement was one of the main, toxic behaviours contributing to my mental disease. It would happen so fast that I was rarely conscious that I was doing it. I believe that it caused me to miss out on some amazing adventures, opportunities and incredible, meaning-of-life relationships. I was so judgemental about myself that I could let one mistake fester for years. It didn't even have to be a big, hurtful mistake for me to dwell on it over and over. Because I set an impossible standard for myself, I would berate myself for simply forgetting to fill out swimming lesson forms on-time, to return a phone call or ordering almond milk in my coffee.

One, well intentioned, simple conversation could lead to hours of lost sleep and counter-productive stress. I would repeat the entire interaction and play them over in my head, analyzing how I might have been perceived. Without a doubt, I would never intend to criticize or hurt another person in any way, but if I felt that I had been misunderstood, the self-judgement was relentless and disabling.

Once I had zoned in on judgement, I was aware it was a chronic habit. Since my teens, I would physically feel the effects of perceived judgement from others. Not as intense as my Stephen Avenue story at the beginning of the book, but just walking down the street, every person I passed seemed to have a silent judgement that I let myself absorb.

When in a crowd (which I would often avoid), it was like I was being pinched over and over. It was like I was being (literally) attacked by a swarm of wasps. Thinking of it now, I'm impressed that:

1. I didn't have social anxiety
2. On the outside I was able to appear "normal"

A therapist I visited once said something to me that stuck: The judgments that you are putting on yourself are way worse than others would. 80% of the population think of themselves, 99.9% are thinking of themselves. Knowing this might be true was enough to shift my mindset and the process of banning any form of judgement (on others or myself) became easier.

I haven't done the research, but I would wager a month of Chai lattes that women are likely to be more judgemental than men. And are more likely to feel judgement from others. Women seem to have more rules for themselves. It is like we have unspoken laws that we need to abide by to navigate through this world. As adolescents, we are blessed with a ridiculous breeding ground for judgement! We helplessly watch our bodies radically, uncontrollably grow and change. There is so much room for self-judgement: too tall or short, a picky eater, good student, boob development, athletic ability, mental stability, where we live, what to wear, dog or a cat person and many other comparisons. As we get older, add sex to the mix and career choice, whether or not to become a parent, and then choosing between that career or staying at home, or paving your own path. Of course, visible signs of aging show up not long after. The possible comparisons are endless and so can then, the self judgement.

On a ski trip to Panorama, BC in 2019, my friend Andrea and I had an in depth conversation about judgment and how it can weave it's way into every fibre of our lives. Though we were opposite students growing up, we both relentlessly judged ourselves and felt judged by others. Andrea excelled at academics, but even though her marks were 90%, she had a constant feeling of under delivering at all times. Andrea told me that she remembered feeling the judgement from family and friends too. Friends would joke, "how come you only got 97%, not 100%?"

The majority of the time it was said in a teasing and loving way, but she felt criticized and judged. She took it as she had underperformed even though it was meant to be taken as over-performance. No matter how good, if we get trapped in a "worst critic" mode, we will never, ever be good enough.

Andrea shared a powerful story with me about a conflict in her social circle that played out over social media. It was clear to her that a friend was angry with her, but hadn't reached out to have a conversation about it. Instead, the wrath was published on social media. Andrea has been a facilitator at work for about two years for leadership in the workplace and the role of judgement was discussed a lot. She credits this experience to being able to view this hurtful virtual stream from a more knowledgeable perspective. A situation that had the potential to cause her great distress and have a negative effect on her work/ home life was viewed from a place of understanding and she chose to consciously try not to judge her friend's actions.

We both agreed that we thought it was a probability that those most judgemental of us are possibly doing so to ensure deflection of any comments directed their way. Also, that it is a brilliant tactic to shift judgement to others to provide a reprieve from our own self judgement. We also both believe that when we judge others, we judge ourselves. When we stop, it can be replaced with kindness, empathy and understanding.

Unless we actually know the truth, the whole truth and get to know them, how can we make a considered decision about anyone else? There are people in our daily lives and all around the world that we won't see again or have an opportunity to have a conversation with. We might see how they look or listen to another's opinion but if we personally don't have a chance to know them or hear their story or rationalizations, can we ever truly understand what their life is like? I started to become aware of habitual judgements I was making and ask myself if they were mostly based on false information.

The feeling when I decided to make a considered effort to ban judgement of others from my life: Freedom.

You know when the hardest time to not judge others was? While driving! It took a lot of practice and frequently talking to myself out loud in the car to 90% cure myself. Staying patient and being non-judgemental when in traffic is a skill! Really, we have zero clue what is happening in another driver's world. Andrea, shared a story during our Pano conversation about completely losing her patience on a guy after his car hit hers. She felt awful after getting so angry, but what he couldn't know was that there had been 2 other car accidents in her immediate family in the past 2 weeks. Three car accidents in 3 weeks! She was reacting from that place. It wasn't about the other driver necessarily.

Note: *This next trick has been amazing for patience and calm while driving...*

Fab Mind Trick

#9. Feel. See. Hear.

To get yourself grounded and your brain focused on the present moment:

- Stop what you are doing and focus on your body and your surroundings.
- What are 3 things you can feel? Your toes in your shoes. Air coming through your nostrils, wind on your face.
- Then focus on things you can see. A tree, bird, your hands in your lap.
- Then focus on things you can hear. A tv on, creaks of the house, a dog barking, traffic, kids playing, the wind in the trees.

There is no limit to how many things you choose to feel, see and hear or often or how long you do it. I find it works every time and has been my #1 go-to for bringing me into the present.

I knew judgement didn't have any validity or serve me in any way. Judging others wouldn't get me further ahead or make me happy one tiny bit. I handled judgement the same way as comparison to make it simple. I became aware when I was doing it and stopped it.

Note: FAB Mind Trick #2 STOP and #5 Positive Affirmations were useful when breaking the judgement habit.

Jealousy to Admiration

I'm good enough, I'm smart enough, and gosh darn it, people like me!
- Stuart Smiley, Saturday Night Live

Have you ever been a total bitch to a woman/friend that you Love and admire? Said things or given advice that is unsupportive and maybe a bit sabotage-y? Ever found it hard to be nice to the most dynamic woman in the room? You know the one - timeless, confident, witty, physically outstanding, beautiful hair, successful, amazing clothes, and she's actually nice and sweet and KIND! She is also driven, is sought out for her priceless advice, has tons of energy, creates her own wealth, has a small part in a new movie (and did I mention she is classy, friendly, beautiful, simply perfect?).

Low self esteem **was keeping the exact woman I aspired to be like at arm's length.** I was in awe at how easy these women made it look. And their confidence made me sad. Sad, because I wasn't there and desperately wanted to be. When I spent time around women like this, I became acutely aware of my insecurities. Interactions weren't genuine because I would constantly compare myself instead of being in the moment with them, enjoying their company and allowing myself to have meaningful conversations.

I wasn't listening and learning.
I was internally comparing and judging myself.

I would present myself as confident and truly wanted to be fully engaged, but I couldn't seem to fight the overwhelming emotion of envy. It was so exhausting!

I would look at these seemingly perfect, flawless women - their success, passion, lifestyle, contentment with being a homemaker or a business owner or a waitress or a sales woman and I would analyze their mannerisms and habits. I would wish I was more like them. I could almost physically feel a wall slide up to protect me (or try to) from myself. My own abusive assault, and comparisons would leave me feeling lost, deflated and overwhelmed by the effort I would have to exert to achieve what they have. Even though we are both human and perfectly imperfect, I would put them on one side (the sunny, exotic, beachy side) and I'd be on the other (the lonely, desolate, dusty side). I was so desperate to find my purpose that, a few times, I tried the approach of adopting their passions and interests. That never worked.

It felt kind of like I was dating someone who was constantly reminding me I was not good enough, pointing out the ways my friends were more attractive and fun to be around. Being envious of others was yet another way I was staying in an abusive relationship with myself and made social situations no fun. I would usually drink too much, taking me farther away from who I wanted to be.

Did I have the energy to change this perception? I was aware and acknowledged I was doing it, but some habits are harder to break than others. And once I found out who Carey really is and let her rock unattended, would they like me? Would I be rejected (gross!), would my heart get broken and could I recover from those if it happened? So I had to figure out how to become ok with that too.

I had to figure out how to be comfortable with being uncomfortable.

Once I defined the exact problem (I'm super jealous of other women's accomplishments, contentment, confidence), I was excited to try to stop it. I let myself have a tiny pity party for the wasted time and energy on things that weren't serving me or helping me find who I was, and then my awareness started to shift.

Note: FAB Mind Trick #8 - Zip Yourself Up - is fabulous to use when feeling jealous or in comparison-mode.

Locus of Control

About 10 years ago, I met one of these glorious women that I fully admire. My ridiculously fabulous and ambitious friend Ashley and I volunteered together for a local sport organization. We also facilitated the Roots of Empathy Program[5] together. She was the perfect fit for the ideal woman I would have been super jealous of. Ashley has become a life-long friend and mental wellness supporter. She saw in me what I wasn't seeing, genuinely took every opportunity to spark my dreams and didn't give me a chance to feel jealous.

---

5 What is Roots of Empathy? rootsofempathy.org

She made me blush a lot (accepting praise from those you admire helps here too), but she also had me start to realize my true potential. When we saw each other, Ashley would not let me get away without planting a seed of confidence. She taught me that other women can be super fabulous AND want you to be your best, fabulous self too. They don't want you to hide or shy away from the wonderful craziness that is you. She showed me what the word "tribe" means and that other women can, without a doubt, be our biggest, truest, loyal fans!

Fab Mind Trick

#10. Tribe.

"Love grows brains!"

- Roots of Empathy Program

Spend time with your people, your tribe. Like-minded friends that see, respect, and get you. Your tribe is filled with those who know that you are human and aren't perfect but Love you and laugh with you anyway. You've been through the ugly together and you're still in. Those who on your team even when you are not in the room (got your back, don't talk behind it). These are people (or pets) in your life that are your tribe. What I have learned, it is NEVER TOO LATE to join, create and be a part of a tribe. As we evolve, our relationships evolve. Find a new tribe if you need one. Nourish your tribe relationships.

Volunteer at a community event or join a group or a class. Pay attention to events going on around you and that catch your attention. Trust your gut, follow a spark and meet your people. Quality, not quantity.

Ashley is an Integrative Health Coach & an exercise physiologist at the University of Calgary. I credit her confidence in me as one of the reasons I was able to write a book.

Our conversations would focus on mental wellness and admiration for others who are doing amazing work. Sometimes her adventurous and compassionate husband Mike joins us and we share inspiring stories and programs where people are blazing new trails. No matter how tired we were or how crazy our weeks had been, we leave feeling energized and enlightened bursting with ideas of how to make a better world.

Finding a relationship built on mutual respect with Mike and Ashley to talk to was a lifeline for me. I could trust to share everything I was feeling, knowing that they knew it was not coming from a place of feeling the victim or self pity, but more, "isn't this weird/interesting?" They understood that even though I had a great life, I was often frustrated because my autopilot thoughts were negative, abusive, unsupportive and not helpful AT ALL. They listened with compassion and were non-judgemental. They asked questions to clarify and get a sense so the conversation could evolve. Conversations like these can change the world, people!

When the topic of my book came up one night so did the underlying issue of the abusive relationship. Ashley told me about "The element of Locus of Control"[6].
There are 2 types: Internal and external.

1. Internal. The belief that YOU can make things happen. It is a feeling of empowerment - that your actions can impact the outcome.
2. External. When your locus of control is, or moves to be, external (outside of your control), you feel that things are happening TO YOU.

Locus of control can shift over our lifetime. Injuries, traumatic events and heartbreak can shift the control, but you alway have the power to bring it back to you!

Our brains have the power to create negative thoughts
so they also have the power to generate positive ones.

Those who seem to have a more optimistic attitude find that they have the resources to overcome negative states when they present themselves. We are born with certain temperament traits (Page ?), but we can train the brain, over time, to shift the way we want it to. If we genuinely feel that we do have control, that our actions create successes in our lives, the more likely we are to try new things and take risks to make our dreams come true.

---

6 verywellmind.com/what-is-locus-of-control-2795434

More and more research is coming out about humans and our habits. So much of what we do is not really in our conscious mind. We rely on cues and triggers that are not in our conscious thought. How much of what builds us up or tears us down comes from conscious thought? How much of our well being comes from subconscious thought? It is fascinating to think that:

Our subconscious thoughts could be
setting us up daily for failure.
That was me.
That is why I wrote this book.

We can also have subconscious actions. We humans are creatures of habit, habits that have been formed over time. How we cope and respond to daily stress in our lives has a huge impact on our happiness.

Example: The Big Mac Effect.
If you choose to eat it, how will you feel after?
If you know you will feel gross after having a Big Mac
but you eat it anyway, it is a good indication that you
might want to change the habit.

Let's say that you are having a really tough day. What is the first thing you do for help? Do you phone a friend and have a meaningful conversation? Do you drive home and experience road rage? Do you go for a drink? Or maybe 10? How about going home and binge eating a bunch of junk food? Do we choose helpful strategies or self harm behaviours? Can they be an abusive habit? Yup. Can we reprogram our brains by changing the action? Absolutely. Is it easy? Absolutely not!

The cue will be the same: It's late and I'm tired and I want comfort. And the action still has to have a similar effect of providing comfort (instead of a bag of chips or a glass of wine, have tea and a bath), but we HAVE THE POWER to retrain our brains.

With Judgement, a chapter of my book, Ashley, Mike and I started wondering about how much of a role do our HABITS play in processing judgement? Whether it be self judgement or perceived judgement?

If we feel judged as a parent by a friend, how do we process and/or respond? Do you have self sabotage thoughts (she doesn't like me anymore, I'm a bad parent, I would never get that job) or would you make the phone call and clear it up. The key here is to feel empowered that we (YOU) can and will make the right decisions to make yourself feel better, live happier, Love the life that you are creating. Change the script from, "I need someone else to tell me what to do or can I do," to a more empowering version of, "I will get information from others I trust and will make the best decision for myself by myself."

Once I started to ditch jealousy and choose to embrace and trust other amazing, successful, beautiful women, I started to thrive personally. Now it is natural for me to admire and feel grateful to have these amazing people part of my life. It truly is magical.

11. "I am Magic!"

A word that describes how I want to feel everyday is MAGICAL.

With this trick, I use the word magical, but pick any word that resonates with you.

- Pick the word for you. Say to yourself, (saying it out loud can be more powerful): "I am MAGICAL!" I'll say my name sometimes for an even greater impact (even writing this is making me smile a little because I feel a bit silly but it works). "Carey, you are magical! Today I'm going to be magical, feel magical and scatter beautiful magic to others I meet!"
- Say it again and pay attention to how your body feels.
- Repeat as many times as you want and to feel the word has made an impact.

This is a trick I still use daily because I can physically FEEL my body change. Each cell seems to adjust to the Love and possibility of being magical!

Note: I sometimes took it deeper:

"I am magical. And everything that I am going through right now and everything I have experienced and done in my past, the way my brain works, the way I've grown up, ALL of these experiences are helping me to be the person I need to be to help the people I Love the most. I am magical and my unique experience makes me the perfect person to help others navigate their lives while on this earth. To help them live, create, find purpose, live adventurous, content lives and realize their amazing, unique gifts."

3. Trust

Deciding what tattoo I wanted fit beautifully into the healing journey. For Christmas when I was 35, my fantastic sister gave me a gift certificate for my very first tattoo. It took some serious self reflection to decide what I would painfully have needled on my body forever. The word 'trust' came firmly behind my first choice 'thank you'. After the tattoo artist's input and seeing the sketch, I knew TRUST was my word. It was perfect. 'Thank you', I realized, was directed more to the universe, forces outside of me. 'Trust' is a word that resonated as something I aspired to live daily. I wanted to wrap myself up in trust and learn how to have it be a part of my whole being.

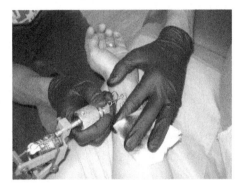

> "Don't make decisions based on FOMO (fear of missing out), find JOMO (joy of missing out)."
>
> *- Brené Brown*

I knew it wasn't going to be easy but I needed to find a way to rewire my brain to trust. To trust myself, my actions, my intentions, my choices, that I'm exactly where I'm meant to be. Trust that I will make the right decisions for myself and my family. Trust the right people will come into my life but more importantly into my son's life. To trust the journey, the exact place where I am in life, that I never miss a boat I was meant to be on. Trust my past, where I grew up, the friendships (a lot formed because of basic geography) and that the most significant ones were there to teach me imperative lessons. Trust my instincts, my parenting decisions, the school system, traveling the world and the universe. Trust that life is full of good and bad and beautiful and sad, and that we won't just survive, but thrive and embrace the adventure.

Trusting my physical safety was a huge priority too. To be able to lock the doors at night simply because that is what you do before you go to bed, not because I felt scared that something bad was going to happen to me. Or worse, to my family and I wouldn't be able to protect them. I had to trust and feel that I was safe in my own house or I would surely go insane.

Unfortunately, the empath in me let my imagination feel what it would be like to be physically attacked. My home is the place where I wanted to allow myself to relax and feel safe but my mind kept taking me to places where I felt violated and a feeling that I was constantly someone's prey. It was a terrible place to be.

I Love that it was a Saturday Night Live skit that first introduced me to positive affirmations. FAB Mind Trick #5 has been great in rewiring my brain to trust.

The following was customized for a young person in my life and I have used it often myself:

- I am safe
- My house is safe
- My community is safe
- My country is safe
- I can handle anything that comes my way
- I am strong and powerful
- I hold my head up high and walk proud
- My body is strong
- I can defend myself

Deepak and Oprah 21-Day Meditation Experience

I evolve every time I do a 21-Day Meditation[7] created by Oprah Winfrey and Deepak Chopra. These have been significant in rewiring and healing my mind and helping me to trust in all aspects of my life. Each day builds on the next and gives me something to focus my intentions on. The meditations are even more amazing because they can be accessed in the app anytime, anywhere. Day 1 through day 21 all have a purpose and work together. About 3 times a year, they offer one for free for about a month. Each day is available for 5 days. After about 27 days, the experiences are sold on their website. I have bought 2 so I can listen to them anytime: 'Manifesting True Success' and 'Desire and Destiny' and I'll be buying the one they have offered for free during the 2020 pandemic, 'Hope in Uncertain Times'.

On Day 9 of 'Hope in Uncertain Times' (How to Truly Trust Yourself!!), Deepak blew my mind. He said:

"When the realization dawns that inner awareness can take care of life, there is an end to struggle, self doubt, pessimism, anxiety and lack of trust."

- Deepak Chopra

Awareness! The end to lack of trust!! The end to anxiety and self doubt! He explains that trust based on an unchanging core of consciousness is different from our conventional understanding of trust. It isn't trusting that other people will do and say what you expect of them. Basing trust on the expectation of permanence (because lives are always changing and unpredictable) from outside is unrealistic and can leave a feeling of doubt and fear. Real trust must be based on something unchanging and permanent so therefore, reliable.

---

7 21-Day Meditation Experience - Google Play App Store

We can only find that foundation inside ourselves. It is important that we recognize our true strength, value and ability for what is. Then we won't depend on outside sources for our inner trust and strength (authoritarian figures we give our trust to protect or save us). The trust we have in ourselves will be unshakeable.

Deepak suggested that a lot of us deal with our fears by trying to defend against them. Many of us chose external things that we think will help like money, possessions and status, but the external approach won't really help. We have to feel SECURE INSIDE to feel totally safe. After I got my first tattoo (Page ?), Deepak's logic helped me to trust and feel safer than I have ever felt.

> *"The most secure person is not someone who has the best defences but someone who needs NO DEFENCES."*
>
> *- Deepak Chopra*

If, on the inside, we are calm and secure, it is more difficult to disrupt the peaceful feeling. It can feel difficult for me when I watch the news, especially at night, if I let myself be constantly bombarded by sad or violent stories of suffering, neglect and hateful conflict.

Deepak explains in one meditation that, "security comes from within us. This is the most basic level of self empowerment. With a foundation of safety and security, we don't let anxiety over worst case scenarios fester and let terrible events (loss of someone we love …) that may NEVER happen consume us."

"We can have the best security system, high walls and watch dogs and still not feel safe.

- Deepak Chopra

Sleep

I Love sleep! But I've been a terrible sleeper for most of my life. It seems impossible to turn my brain off, so sleep has always been a cause of anxiety for me. I envy anyone who can turn off their brain and sleep in cars and planes and hammocks! I've always wanted to be a person who could fall asleep within seconds of head hitting pillow. That would be pure bliss! If I go 2 or 3 nights without having a good night sleep, my emotions are not to be trusted and I can feel crazy. This is why sleep is always a priority for me.

I have tried hundreds of things but these are a few that work the best:

*   Deepak 21-Day Meditation Experience
*   Guided meditations where someone talking. Tons on YouTube.
*   Visualize an empty, black chalkboard. Just black. And then focus on completely relaxing my jaw (crazy how the jaw holds stress). When my mind wanders, bring back to black.
*   Hylands 'Calm' chewables.
*   Read. From a book, not a screen. Not scary or too heavy.
*   Close my eyes, focus on relaxing my body and repeat the words "thank you" over and over.
*   Squeeze and Release! FAB Mind Trick #12...

#12. Squeeze and Release.

- Start at your toes and squeeze them, crunch them up.
- Hold for a few breaths and then release.
- Then point your toes and do the same. Hold, breathe and release.
- Work your way up the whole body. Make a fist, hold, release, tighten your ab muscles, hold, release. I squeeze my butt cheeks together and squish up my face too.

There aren't any rules. Where is your body feeling stress? The idea is to release any tension, distract the mind and hopefully exhaust the body and relax enough to fall asleep.

Medication

I almost left medication out of this book. Mostly because of the conflicted relationship I have with it. I hate, Love, am confused by, am scared of, don't want it, find it improves my quality of life, find it hard to explain, forget to take it, can't live without it, Google it, ignore it, recommend it, am embarrassed that I need it.

I decided it was time to TRUST the process, not fight against something proven. Was it possible medication might help me feel safe, calm the anxiety and give my mind the opportunity to breathe so I could prioritize and get help? Deciding to include medications as part of my healing process was scary. They might work but they might not. I knew they could actually make me feel worse or create new issues, and it takes a lot of communication and appointments with a doctor. It could be a life-long commitment.

When a nurse told me that I had mild postpartum depression when my son was about 2 months old, I felt a huge sense of relief. It finally gave me a legitimate reason to talk about what was going on in my head. The combination of extreme empathy for things I could not control, low self esteem, my active imagination and loss of direction affected my life negatively and aggressively. I was constantly exhausted and it depleted my creative energy. My brain literally kept me up at night.

Postpartum depression was a gift. It let me allow myself to try medication. I had almost immediate and amazing results. The struggle eased and the fog lifted. I have found meds to be one of the best tools in this journey, but also the most frustrating and discouraging.

It was beautiful Marcie who changed my mind about putting medication in this book. We met in the fall of 2019 at the women's retreat that focused on letting go of the past. Medication was not yet a chapter in this book. At our vegan breakfast on the first morning, Marcie sat down directly across from me and placed her prescription bottle on the table. With extreme confidence and almost buzzing with excitement, she opened the bottle and took out what I recognized as Vyvanse, a commonly used drug for those with ADD (Attention Deficit Disorder). "Is that Vyvanse?" I asked. "Yup it is!" she said pumped up. "It is my lifesaver and I never forget to take it."

Later in the weekend, I asked if she would share her story with me. Her nonchalant, almost "I'm proud of my medication" stance was inspiring to me. The more we talked about the benefits of her medication, the more grateful I was for meeting her. My feelings of shame towards taking meds began to disappear.

Marcie was 49 years old when she was referred to the Bariatric clinic to lose weight. She had been screened for the program and part of the initial process was to fill out a questionnaire with her doctor. At this point she was seeing a therapist once a week for anxiety and depression (which can be very common with a diagnosis of ADD) and was being treated with medication. Her relationship with food was abusive - she compared it to self harm. "Some people cut themselves, I ate and ate to a level where it became abusive.". She told me that when she ate, she couldn't hear the negative voices in her head. My whole body got the shivers when she said that. For me food and drink have always been a coping strategy. Tasting, chewing, crunching, dipping, the noises. The actions and noises of eating are glorious distractions for a brain that won't stop thinking, processing, questioning, solving. Our senses are triggered when we eat and it helps the constant nagging, insistent, spiralling brain. Sadly, the reprieve of eating (same as drinking) doesn't last very long. Unless you keep eating.

It was during this initial process to the Bariatric clinic when she found out that she is an "ideal candidate for the program but she needs to be treated for her ADD."

Marcie takes her Vyvanse everyday. She works from home but has learned to adjust her meds when she is needed at the office where there are more distractions.

It took my postpartum depression for me to finally justify going on medication. When I did, I noticed positive effects immediately! This was unexpected because I had read it can take up to 3 months to work properly. I had low expectations and was pleasantly surprised. It was a gift and a relief. But it also made me feel weak and embarrassed - that I couldn't do it on my own that I needed medication to keep myself balanced. I didn't want to be dependent on unnatural remedies. But because the effects were so instant, I knew that I needed to change my relationship with medication.

Medication is amazing and unpredictable and acts so differently for each of us. I don't give all the credit to medication, but it definitely helped. In less than a week I noticed I had a clearer, more patient mind to work through issues. Never did I think a medication would be a solution to helping me accept me for who I am or develop a more positive self image, but they have been a huge, unexpected (yet unwanted) ally for me.

Continual communication with doctors, honest talks with trusted, nonjudgemental friends and family, along with trusting yourself are imperative to make informed decisions about meds. I've had to come to peace with the fact that it might be a lifetime of changes and adjusting. This might not ever be easy for me. I'm telling myself this as much as I'm telling you right now: trust yourself and your body to know how to heal when you give it the right tools. Sometimes it takes a little dose and you might notice relief right away. Sometimes it will be larger doses and a lot more patience. Every brain and body chemistry is different. Managing medication is not easy, but from my own experience and many stories from others I've talked to, it is definitely worth it!

I don't want to be a person who needs medication to survive on this earth, but, fabulous reader, I know I'll probably be taking some sort of prescription medication my whole life. For me, the positive has definitely outweighed the negative.

Even with the proper medication, I use several FAB Mind Tricks daily, and #13 has been amazing to calm my mind and body, help me feel grounded and clear any negative energy that I'm not even aware is affecting me...

Fab Mind Trick

#13. Clear Your Energy.

Use this anytime you are feeling anxious. I often use this one before socializing in big groups, when feeling stressed while driving and whenever I am feeling overwhelmed. You can do it sitting or standing.

- Take 3 deep breaths.
- With your flat palm facing your body, put your right palm up by your left shoulder.

- Swipe up and down rapidly the length of your whole torso, while taking quick exhales of breaths with each swipe. Do the same thing on the opposite side. After doing the torso, you can do both arms, legs, back - whole body if you want.

If you are feeling negative energy from someone specific or feeling you are attaching emotions to someone that isn't serving you in your life, you can imagine the breaking of the joined energy while doing this.

Peace, Love, Therapy

Did you know the average number of sessions with a therapist is 4 to 6? That's how many sessions it takes to solve a current life issue or help someone feel they are able to conquer their struggle. This is depending on the depth of the trauma of course, but it doesn't take long to start the unraveling of a very messy bowl of spaghetti noodle brain! I was skeptical of the benefits at first but, every time, I am AMAZED what an hour of therapy can accomplish!

It is estimated that before Canadians reach 40 years of age, 1 in 2 have, or have had, a mental illness.[8]

I have been to several amazing therapists in the past 20 years. Words like, "tortured", "abusive", "non-stop", "relentless",

---

[8] The Centre for Addiction & Mental Health. camh.ca

"racing" have been used to describe how my brain works. I've heard often, "Wow, you've got a lot going on up there!" Hearing a professional's opinion scared and surprised me, but I also felt relief in feeling UNDERSTOOD by someone else! I was feeling so trapped in my own head and I was struggling and confused daily. It is so glorious when, finally, someone gets it, empathizes and (the best) ensures there is hope for me. I remember the first time I realized I wouldn't have to struggle forever. The sounds of angels singing filled my entire skull preventing any negative thoughts to penetrate this new, protective force field. The heavy, evil, thick and dark clouds that sat permanently in my brain opened up to huge, billowy, gentle white ones. Letting the amazing healing power of the sun blaze through. That is the power of hope. Hope that I am normal, hope what I am experiencing is normal and hope there are many, proven solutions that will help. That was a glorious day.

Note: Normal is one of my least favourite words in our language because I don't believe there is such a thing. However, it is one that is understood by most as meaning typical, usual, expected.

Recently I found myself in a place where I knew I needed some time with a therapist.

I was voted off the island.

There wasn't a tribal council. No respectful conversations for clarity and understanding. After six years of being a solid, committed, caring, nurturing, call-me-anytime-because-you-are-always-a-priority friend, I was cast off and left stunned and confused. I wasn't given a minute of explanation or even three seconds to try and defend myself. Years of history and evidence of being a dedicated BFF were discarded, forgotten and completely erased. After being intentionally and publicly shunned in front of a very respected social group, I was feeling humiliated, misunderstood and devastated.

In the days and weeks following, the shock, confusion, lack of respect for the friend I had been and sadness consumed me. My mind spent hours trying to solve the ache my whole body felt but I was unable to comprehend any of it. I wasn't told what I had done or said. Of course I speculated about the cause, but I didn't know their reasons, thoughts or perception. I obviously screwed up somewhere, but nothing I came up with could justify the way I was being treated. I've had my share of conflicts and I'm accustomed to having private, honest, respectful conversations when misunderstandings arise.

I think not having a voice was one of the hardest things for me to overcome. I wanted understanding, answers and to defend the relationships, but it was clear it wasn't going to happen. When conversations were taking place without me, but about me (basically voting me off the island), I knew I had to find a way to trust what was happening and let it go.

This event happened when I was 46. Life was good. I was working, I was happy in my marriage, my son was figuring his life out, my family was healthy. But this knocked me off kilter. I would try and focus on all the positives around me but there was a root of sadness that had burrowed in and refused to budge. I'd never been treated with such disrespect from someone I trusted with my whole heart. If I did mess up, was misunderstood, showed weakness or did/said something that offended, I trusted my heart was looked after, considered... safe. The situation was taking up valuable mind space, had a ripple effect on several relationships and started showing up, uninvited, in my dreams.

I diagnosed myself with emotional PTSD when I realized I was starting to doubt the integrity of other important friendships.

It was time for therapy.

Starting the process of seeing a new therapist requires patience. I phoned our local mental health clinic, spent a half hour talking with an intake worker and made an appointment for 5 weeks out. I was a bit discouraged about the wait, but in the past I have come to discover solutions often present themselves between appointments.

Note: There are therapists that specialize in trauma and grief. To help us forgive ourselves. For doing our best at the time. For doing what we had to do to survive.

I have seen dozens of therapists over the years. Female, male, young and old. They all had their time and place in my life. Some I have paid for (some have a sliding scale), but most have been free. Alberta Health Care is excellent at making mental health a priority and I am continually grateful for the services I can access. I have even found sessions held over the phone can be very productive.

My latest sessions helped me shift my internal voice. Offending others is inevitable but anyone who knows me, knows I would never do anything with ill intention. If the relationship is one that is a priority, conversations will be had. We took time to answer the question, "has anything positive come out of it?" The answer is yes. It has strengthened my relationship with my husband and my son, I have a better understanding of who I am, it gave me a huge springboard to evolve and a new appreciation for relationships I am proud of.

Note: TRUST that the hardest things are teaching you the greatest lessons and providing you with experience you might need one day to help someone you Love more than yourself.

I suffered a long time with low self-esteem before I realized that there are TONS of resources in Canada. Thousands of people and organizations make it their life mission to help others live their best lives. From family doctors to personal trainers to chiropractors to podcasts to books to dentists to phone hotlines to workshops to nutrition experts to psychologists to innovations in healthcare. At one point in my life I was so overwhelmed that I couldn't seem to find the energy to look for solutions, but after meeting my husband (who made me want to be my best self so I could be the best partner to him) and the birth of my son, I started to research options to get to the root of my dis-ease. To even start the journey to a full recovery felt unsurmountable. All of my random negative thoughts, layers of insecurities and constantly spinning brain (picking up so much more information each day) made it very difficult to think of or plan for a future.

My mind is often blown in therapy (I love that!!) and many times sessions completely exceeded my expectations. The process enlightens me to who I am and to show respect to that person. I've had to answer the questions necessary to know and believe in myself. I learned that I am very open minded and it is essential for me to seek to understand all sides of a situation. My brain automatically considers and feels empathy for everyone involved. My thoughts are 50,000 shades of grey. I'm not capable of black & white thinking. Believe me, sometimes I wish I could! I think life might be more simple.

Therapy is not just for the mentally unwell. Ongoing sessions with a variety of professionals have been a lifesaver for me. Fighting judgemental voices? Want more sincere conversations with your partner? Having parental guilt? Trouble sleeping? Can't make sense of a significant moment or your emotions? Looking for a fair take on a situation? If you are struggling to sort it out, a commitment of only 4-6 hours can be a game changer.

Leading into my fifth therapy session, I was 80% sure we would decide not to book another session. This is because I felt 80% better than when I started. My whole mindset about getting voted off the island had changed. Therapy helped me to see obstacles as a gift, reevaluate my friendships and focus more time on my family.

A little therapy tip: Do not hold back! Be completely honest, get to the hardest stuff and dig deep. I believe that we get so much more out of each session when we get to the GOOD STUFF (hard, ugly, embarrassing, shameful, hurtful, gross …) right away.

#14. Ground Yourself.

My beautiful friend, Sandy, introduced me to one of the best grounding experiences I've ever had. We are pulling on the strength from our earth and the energy from our sky.

- Lay down and get extremely comfortable.
- Close your eyes, put your arms to your sides and turn your palms to face the earth.
- Take 3 deep, cleansing (imagine pulling in the positive and breathing out all negative) breaths.
- The next inhale, imagine pulling in all of the love and strength from our earth (Mother Earth). Feel the solid strength fill you.

- On your exhale, pull in the light, energy and healing properties from our powerful sky and sunshine.
- Repeat this until you feel you have cleared your negative thoughts and feelings and are now filled up with a solid foundation and the positive energy.
- Then I imagine clean, healing water coming down on me. All over, around and through me. As it passes through, I visualize it takes all of the toxins, grief, guilt, shame, regret (anything you don't feel is serving you anymore) with it.

Perfectly Imperfect

At a women's retreat in Spring 2019, we focused our energy on how to let go of anything from our past that wasn't helping us move forward. We were encouraged to see the gift or lesson in each situation, and to give up hoping that the past can be any different. The possibility of this mindset being a reality for me and the feeling of freedom that would bring, inspired me to put all of my energy into the process. I was determined to live life in the present and not let my past regrets, failures, insecurities, and shame define me. It is an amazing gift we can give ourselves: to live life in the present, to act and make choices from the place we are in and not from the disappointments or fears of past decisions. To know that what you choose now is the best choice and it won't be a cause of stress for you now or in the future. To embrace that we are:

Perfectly Imperfect, Baby!

I was so afraid to make decisions because of the pressure I would put on myself to make the RIGHT one. Feeling scared that I'd make the wrong decision, even if it seemed simple, caused me hundreds of hours of mental struggle. Parenting choices have been the most stressful because I was so desperate to be a good, ...NO, not just a good, but a fantastic, amazing, decisive mom!! The perfect mom. In fact, it was my son that ultimately inspired me to get out of the abusive relationship with myself. Becoming a mom forced me to put my mental health as top priority. I had to take the pressure off of myself and be MY best version of his mom. Not a perfect mom - that doesn't exist.

Emotional Literacy

Our emotions, all of them are, "not good or bad. They are not right or wrong. They are part of who we are."

- Mary Gordon, Roots of Empathy Founder

The best and most rewarding volunteer position I've held was my 6 years as an instructor for the, Canadian Founded, Roots of Empathy Program.

The Roots mission is to build more caring, peaceful, and civil societies by raising levels of empathy in children. I know for certain I would have been easier on myself as a new mom if I'd instructed this program before becoming a parent.

During the school year, I would visit the same classroom 27 times to deliver the program. We would cover 9 themes from October to June, each theme relevant to the development of humans from birth to 1 year. The super cool part was that a parent and baby, who was 2 to 4 months old when the programs started, would come 9 times - once for each theme! I would have a new family each year and mom and I would meet when she was pregnant and become an empathy teaching team. Week one of each theme, I would visit the class and we would talk about our current theme and how it might relate to our baby right now. When the theme "Crying" was introduced, we would talk about why a baby might cry and what a caregiver could do to help (and how important it is to get help yourself). We would record a list of questions to ask during the family visit. Over the school year, we watched our baby change, grow and reach many amazing milestones.

One of my favourite themes was Emotional Literacy. I was absolutely amazed at how many awesome, huge, unexpected, confusing emotions we can have. It feels as if we put so much pressure on ourselves to always be happy or fine. If we are not happy, then there is something wrong with us.

"Empathy is respect for oneself, understanding and compassion for others, and a sense of responsibility for the world, its citizens and its future."

- Book 'Roots of Empathy' by Mary Gordon

Emotional literacy is the ability to understand our emotions, the ability to listen to others and empathize with their emotions and the ability to express emotions productively. If emotionally literate, we are able to handle emotions in a way that improves our personal power and improves the quality of life around you. This then improves relationships, makes co-operative work possible and allows us to communicate in a calm, respectful manner.

Many of us feel too scared to have hard conversations and tell people how we really feel. Or it is difficult because we don't really understand how it is we are feeling. Or maybe we feel embarrassed to share emotional issues. Our emotions can have a lot of control over us so it can be a very confusing place to be if we don't understand them.

We are all born with thousands of crazy, amazing, changing, raging, confusing, emotions. Some estimate that people have close to 34,000 different emotions! How do we get to a place where all our emotional needs are understood and met? Emotional literacy.

Chart of Human Emotions

This chart blew my mind.[9] The number of emotions humans can feel (and often several at once) is outstanding! It gave me a new respect and more patience for myself.

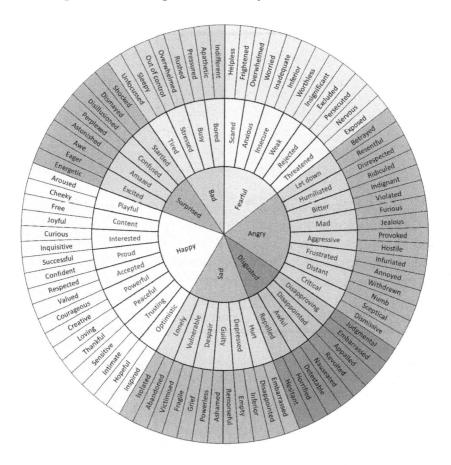

Google, "Wheel of Emotions" to get a larger version or to find resources on how to understand and use this chart.

---

[9] positivepsychology.com/emotion-wheel/ The Emotion Wheel: What is it & how to use it.

What is shocking to me is the lack of positive emotions: HAPPY (yellow) is the only section of the 7 that always feels good. SURPRISED (purple) can produce dramatically different responses depending on the person. Many people I know do not like surprises at all - they feel very uncomfortable. All of these emotions are responsible for every choice we make in life. In reality, we are our emotions.

Without learning about and then sharing, teaching and encouraging others to be OK with all of our human feelings (even the uncomfortable, yucky, gross, sad, disappointed ones), we are bound to misunderstand and feel misunderstood. We have to know it is totally healthy and NORMAL to FEEL EVERYTHING that comes.

If this chart represents us, then negative emotions make up a majority of how we feel and it is very probable that we all will be overcome by anger, anxiety, or depression at least at one point in our lives. What can we do if we find ourselves stuck in the basement (meaning feeling low and stuck and can't get out)? Emotional literacy. Once I started to try and properly identify my emotions and honour them, the less they had control over me. I was able to allow myself to observe, take time to process and then understand what I was feeling, instead of just reacting. I began to be a non-judgemental witness to them.

The first time I really acknowledged my (lack of) emotional literacy was when I became a Mom. There I was, sitting in my hospital bed after (the complete opposite of my birth plan) my amazing son was born, attached to a plug-in breast pump which was unsuccessfully trying to milk me. I had been awake for over 80 hours, was drugged up for pain and recovering from an emergency c-section. I was bloated, disoriented, leaking, sore, still rockin' my mesh hospital undies and I was, for lack of any other word, shell shocked!

It was when we finally got home after the excitement had settled and everyone else resumed their normal routines, that I had an overwhelming, physically disabling realization: I have never felt more scared, ill-equipped and incompetent in my life! This confused me and made me sad because I'd always dreamed of being a mother. It was never the wedding, the dress or the house for me, it was becoming a mom.

How was I, someone who constantly made others needs, opinions, time, and abilities more important than my own, going to be a positive role model to my baby boy? There wasn't a solid foundation of self esteem for me to draw from in those crazy first few months of being a new mom.

I was in DESPERATE need of the same caring and nurturing that I was expected to give my newborn.

Everyday, all day, the responsibility of being a perfect parent smacked me hard and consumed my mind and body. I wasn't at all in a place to enjoy the moment and it was excruciating. Especially because I was fully aware I was doing it!

I would catch myself worrying about explaining consequences (when to give him advice or to just listen?) and if I would help him be confident. I worried about him running out into the road and stressed about navigating him through social situations. He was only 4 days old! There were so many decisions (has he slept enough, soother or no soother, should I incorporate formula, cloth or disposable?) to make and my instincts were nowhere to be found.

This is when I would say that my abusive relationship with myself was taken to another level.

I was desperate to be perfect, but feeling overwhelmed was my baseline. If my patience was low one day, I burnt dinner, forgot something at the grocery store or didn't get to walking the dog, the abuse was relentless: guilt, shame, remorse and self loathing to name a few. I found the feeling of panic was very common (the playground at the Calgary Zoo was a nightmare for me) which had me feeling afraid a lot of the time too. I think most of the fear was because I didn't know what was happening to me. Or if it would ever end?! I felt confused, alone and like I was locked inside my own, abusive brain. I was desperate to be happy and functional, but I didn't know how to explain it to anyone and I didn't want to be a drag. I didn't have an ounce of reserve to navigate, fall, recover and bounce back. Every task, outing, moment of my day was a struggle.

Being completely honest with my local health nurse was step 1, then the daily practice of trust and being in the moment, steps 2 and 3. Becoming emotionally literate has been one of the best educations I could have given myself. My emotions are now a trusted guide instead of an enemy. I feel I am finally a Jedi Master instead of on the dark side!

When we understand our emotions, we become our own trusted mentor. And that Baby, is MAGICAL!

#15. A Good Cry.

When I'm having a hard time understanding what my emotions are trying to tell me, I often feel extremely overwhelmed and stressed. I highly recommend a long, hard and ugly cry. No matter who you are, I whole-heartedly believe a good cry can be extremely helpful for our body to let go of tension. The goal is to feel lighter, clear headed and free!

If it starts on its own, just let it happen for as long as it lasts. If starting to cry doesn't come easily, which doesn't for me (and I'm a crier), a movie can get me started. Have you ever seen the movie, "My Life" with Nicole Kidman and Michael Keaton?

When I have been feeling stress for several days and I can't shake it, I'll plan for a time when I know I'll be in my own space and alone. I Love having my favourite snacks, putting on my most comfy clothes and picking the movie. I make sure I have at least one box of Kleenex close by.

While you are crying, think of things that are making you sad or causing you grief. Let yourself dig deep and feel it all. Cry harder. Visit regrets and heartbreak and the stress you have about money, raising a good kid, what the future will hold. Feel the pain and sadness through your whole body. Don't resist or try to stop - once you are in, take full advantage and heal. Curl in a ball, walk around, lie on the floor or bed - there are no rules. You will know when you are finished. Take deep breaths, sleep, bust out your awesome dance playlist and dance, clean the house, go for a walk, finish the movie - whatever feels right for you.

Note: *Other movies that always worked for me: Dead Poets Society, ET, Steel Magnolias, Benji (any movie separating a dog and it's owner will do it). A music "Cry Playlist" can also do the trick. Songs that remind you of someone, the past, what you let slip away (friends, relationships, opportunities …). Again, be alone so you can be long and loud.*

Temperament

"Temperament is not just a learning style, it is our gut reaction,
our responsiveness to the world on a cellular level."
- Mary Gordon, Author

Studying our temperament traits[10] was also a part of the Roots of Empathy curriculum. These traits determine how we react to situations before we learn to think about reacting. When a baby gets startled or scared, do they laugh or cry? How do they handle a change in schedule? Is their sleep pattern consistent or

---

[10] Book: Your Child is A Person by Alexander Thomas, Stella Chess & Herbert G. Birch

random? I found the study fascinating and now recommend the concept to anyone who will listen, especially parents and caregivers.

The concept is we are all born with our own unique temperament. Born with traits that I would think similar to the Love language concept. They are NOT GOOD or BAD. Nor are they RIGHT or WRONG. Our temperament traits determine how we react to and handle life situations. They provide us with our unique and individual characteristics and play a huge role in who we are.

The 9 Temperament Traits[11]:

- Activity Level
- Adaptability
- Distractibility
- First Reaction
- Intensity
- Mood
- Persistence
- Rhythmicity
- Sensitivity

The temperament traits define who we are and determine with what intensity, and for how long, our emotions run. They can also be a main cause in how we clash with others. The more we know about our own traits, the more we can expect and trust certain reactions in ourselves and help manage them. None of the traits are good or bad or right or wrong, though some can be inconvenient (low adaptability or high intensity). There is a beautiful power in knowing what those we Love might need; often there is a certain type of response that works best for them, but isn't our initial instinct.

---

[11] academia.edu and healthofchildren.com/T/Temperament

It can be hard for caregivers to raise kids with difficult temperament traits. But if they understand why a toddler is reacting to a situation (that they are not doing it to be bad), it might make day to day life easier. I think it is also important for caregivers to know that it is not their fault. Understanding the temperaments of ourselves and others just might help all relationships and even make home life easier to navigate.

Trust Yourself and The Process

A few years into practicing trust, I found I needed to adjust a few daily mindsets. They didn't make a chapter or a FAB Mind Trick, but they made my healing process easier so they are worth a mention. I try to incorporate them into my life everyday and in doing so, life has become much more fun!

They are:

- Be Decisive
- Patience
- Humour
- Live within Your Means
- No Expectations
- Late Bloomer

Be Decisive

This and trust go hand in hand. Take the time you need, talk to the people you need to and make a decision and be decisive. When we are empowered to know that we can and will make the decisions that are best for us (in this moment, on this day), it can only help build confidence. It will be hard, but try not to question the decision after it is made.

Can't make a decision? Try this visual: Find a quite place, be silent and visualize pathways stretching out in front of you. See which ones are open to your journey and which ones aren't. Trust your instincts. A small, open path just might be leading to the huge ocean. Try not to get stuck thinking way too far ahead and stopping before you start (talking yourself out of something).

Patience

"Be patient in the process of healing.
There is no magic pill ... I've tried all of them."

- *Theo Fleury*

This one ain't easy - especially when driving! Patience was a tough one for me to get a hold of. When I was taking fertility drugs, they seemed to rob me of any patience. I was sometimes scared to let myself out in public! I have forgiven myself for taking them and grateful to myself for deciding to not proceed with more invasive procedures. Wowza! THAT, right there!! Huge realization, writing these words! Forgiving myself for taking the steps to get pregnant again (even tho it made me cray for a while) and realizing that, in the end, I made the decision best for my family. No future babies, but mommy wasn't crazy anymore! Writing this book and sharing my story in hopes to help others and healing myself. Magic.

Huge, deep breaths and take time outs if needed has been helpful. I have taken 21 days to work on just *recognizing* when my patience is low and possible triggers.

Fab Mind Trick

#16. Gratitude.

This trick is a treasure and high on the 'Secret to Life' list. In my opinion, gratitude is significant to healing and will pay its weight in pure gold. It is an essential piece. Stopping the negative dialog and only noticing everything I can think of to be grateful for in my day/life has had outstanding effects. I know that some days, it can be hard to be grateful for anything. What I know, there is ALWAYS something to be grateful for. I have found hundreds in a day! For this trick, focus on the tiny things countless times a day.

- I can wiggle my toes. And they don't hurt!
- Cold water AND hot water. At the same source and each tap in my house can do this!
- A loving pet
- A toaster that toasts
- Rain to feed the plants
- Eye sight, hearing, tastebuds
- Your favourite pjs, a chai latte, a green light
- A motivational talking, Mr. Rogers trinket

The possibilities are endless. Being grateful for the small things has been an amazing tool for me.

Humour

Finding the humour in everything (even the most annoying family quirks). Not letting little things become a big deal. Putting things into proper perspective and remember all the tiny things we can be grateful for. Stopping anger and choosing to see a different view. This wasn't a part of my life for a long time and creating a spot in myself for humour has made me a happier person and a better mom/partner.

Live within Your Means

Create a weekly and monthly budget. Get help if you needed Stick to it. For 5 years, I would take cash out every week and put it in an envelope. That was it for the week. When it was gone, I had to wait until Sunday. I didn't use debit or credit (expect for gas which was on budget). I spent less time shopping, learned the value of one dollar and didn't accumulate anything unnecessary.

No Expectations

When one's expectations are reduced to zero, one really appreciates everything one does have.

- Stephen Hawking

Try new things. Don't judge an event or scenario before you try it. I've talked myself out of a lot of things because false expectations got in the way.

Late Bloomer

I absolutely consider myself a late bloomer. In my 20 and 30s I didn't know what my goals were nor what my ambitions and dreams looked like. Even if I did, I'm not sure I'd have had the confidence to pursue them. Trust that you are exactly where you are meant to be.

It is NEVER too late. To be happy, to learn something new, to meet a soul mate, to write a book or a song, to forgive. NEVER TOO LATE. Late Bloomer will be a main topic in my next book. I am 48 and just beginning to realize what I'm capable of. My dad was over 60 when he was hired for his most fulfilling role in his career and provided him with his first ever pension!

It can be very stressful to not know when our time on this earth is going to end. The best way I have found to not think about that is to keep busy doing things that make you feel happy. For some people these are super simple things and for some they travel around the world. There is no good or bad or right or wrong. This belongs to only you and only you know what instinctively makes you happy.

BE KIND. Forgive yourself. Be generous. Be grateful. Embrace aging. Honour everything you've been through. Be decisive. Understand your emotions.

Late Bloomers Unite!

4. Be In The Moment (Always)

"I'm in a hurry to get things done. Oh I rush and rush until life's no fun.
All I really gotta do is live and die, but I'm in a hurry and don't know why."

- Alabama

This is the Jedi Master of Mind Tricks! To be in the present moment at all times, this moment right now and every moment you are awake. I believe this is how we can be our most genuine, decisive, creative selves and hear, feel and trust our instincts. I'm committed to the practice of mastering the art of it for my whole life. Since I made it a priority about 2 years ago, I can tell you that it has gotten easier. An unexpected perk is that I don't feel like I am in a rush and I always seem to have extra time.

My abusive brain was fabulous at, in an instant, flashing me right back to moments from the past where I wished I'd represented myself better. I also loved to worry about events in the future. I'd zone in on the big things like my son's education or my family's (near and far) health but also silly things like if I would find a good parking spot at the airport for my flight in two weeks. I would spend a good chunk of my day mentally trying to solve problems that literally didn't exist.

"Let us not look back in anger, nor forward in fear,
but around in awareness."

- James Thurber, Author

My brain did not mess around when it would pull memories from 30 years ago and they would inflict very negative feelings. They could completely disable my creativity and inspiration in the present. Often, they'd just be flashes of moments, and not necessarily the whole story or situation - the context of the event, long lost.

I knew I was an attentive and loving mom. I certainly know my son had fun, was learning lots and many of our days felt perfect. My son was my priority - he was safe, never harmed and it was a priority for me that he felt understood. Still, I couldn't seem to find forgiveness or compassion for myself in even the small parenting things. Family and friends can attest, I made it a priority to work through all issues and missteps at the time, but I wouldn't remember that part. I didn't and still don't understand why my brain will often torment me with the past.

In the grocery store recently, I saw a woman who we interviewed as a day home provider. When I saw her, my gut clenched and my mind started to race. "Why didn't we choose her? Would she have been a better choice?" What is the point of these thoughts now? It is so over and done. There wasn't an issue at the time and certainly none at present.

Note: FAB Mind Tricks #2 - STOP - and #3 - Do, Don't Think - are very helpful to me in these situations.

Finding ways to stay in the moment and not let the negative dialog have its way was essential to get out of the abusive relationship I was having with myself. My goal was to stop the thoughts before they could inflict any mental and physical stress.

Note: Former Chicago Bulls reporter Mark Vancil shares what he thinks gives Jordan super-human abilities: "Most people struggle to be present. Most people live in fear because we project the past to the future. Michael's a mystic. He's never anywhere else. His gift was not that he could jump high, run fast, shoot a basketball. His gift was that he was completely present. That was the separator."

First I had to let go of the idea that the past could be any different. I'm still struggling with this one but working on it daily. Making the effort to pull my thoughts into the moment has not been easy. When I started, it was a conscious effort about 100 times a day!

One crazy day, about 3 months after I had started practicing being in the moment, I found myself trapped in a memory from the past and I was, FINALLY, able to snap myself out of it! The work of rewiring my brain was having an impact. It surprised and energized me. It will be a lifetime commitment of several reminders and check ins daily to pull myself. I have discovered that driving and when lying in bed are perfect times to practice being in the moment.

I do FAB Mind Trick #9 - Feel, See, Hear - about 6 to 186 times a day. I credit this commitment to being in the moment 50% of the time now.

Fab Mind Trick

#17. Have Fun with Menial Tasks.

Doing daily, necessary menial tasks is the perfect time to practice being in the moment and recognizing things to be grateful for. I enjoy the challenge of finding a way to make them fun!

It is so easy for our minds to focus on the negative when doing chores (even that word makes some cringe). When you sing, play music, make a game of it, the time seems to go by faster. I feel that when we are in the moment, doing your best job at your menial tasks (cleaning, cooking, shovelling, homework …) being happy while doing it can't hurt, so what do you have to lose? And if you have a child watching you are setting them up for a life of positive and fun in the everyday.

I Love to think of John Lennon's lyrics from the song "Beautiful Boy": "Life is what happens to you while you are busy making other plans." I truly believe that if you keep a positive attitude and always do your best job, opportunities will come to you when you least expect it!

Drink

"You'll have to excuse me, I'm not at my best. I've been gone for a month, I've been drunk since I left."

- Home for a Rest by Spirit of the West

In a way, I drink to help me be in the moment. It stops my mind from over analyzing. But, alas, it is always a short-term solution. When I began making my mental health my number one priority, I knew drinking didn't have a place in my life (this includes any recreational drug that can lead to paranoia and lack of motivation).

I wasn't a daily drinker but loved to socialize, have drinks and numb my crazy thoughts. I could always be counted on and available for day drinking (I often joked they were 2 of my favourite words) and I would usually organize a ride home. Yes, it was responsible to have a designated driver, but I did it because I knew I would be having at least 3 or 4 drinks. I LOVED patios and music, pints of beer, meeting new people and, most of all, I loved escaping reality.

Not often, but every once in a while, the pitch black woods panic (described on page 15) would merge with the binge drinking into a perfect storm. Words I would have loved to have used to describe myself like, "graceful" or "classy", bounced off me, dribbled down the street and into the gutter, not knowing if they would ever return again. Nights like those were humbling and VERY hard to recover from.

I knew that too much drink would deplete me mentally and physically. And the older I got, the longer it took me to recover. Being hungover was not a good place for me because it would guarantee a day (or more) full of guilt and self-loathing. It could take my brain 2 to 3 days to recover and be productive again which completely defeated my purpose. Also, I would lose motivation for healthy eating and exercise. To me, it was obvious and necessary: if I wanted to get this book written, alcohol consumption did not have a place in a concentrated, determined journey to self Love and self discovery.

My friend Melissa has been sober for over 5 years and met with me to talk about alcohol as a coping mechanism and how socially acceptable it has become to abuse it. Marketers are very good at portraying drinking as sexy, chic and cool. There are gin, beer and wine advent calendars, fun T-shirts and socks, not to mention happy hour at almost every establishment. We are surrounded by a socially acceptable mentality that all of our fun life events should include alcoholic drinks. Companies and their marketing teams invest hundreds of millions of dollars into creating advertisement to tap (haha) into our deepest feelings.

Both Melissa and I agree there was a point in our lives when we took pride in being the drunk ones. It came to be (or we felt it was) our responsibility to show up and be fun. A saying often heard is, "you can have fun without drinking" but in those days, staying sober never occurred to Melissa or I. We worried we would be less fun, less appealing or make others feel uncomfortable if we weren't drinking. It was a social coping strategy and a habit we fiercely protected. We also both very much agree the feeling doesn't last because a good night always comes to an end. We reflected that too many drinks made it hard to have genuine conversations and took away any authentic credibility. Did we really make a new BFF the night before? Or was it just the drink talking?

Drinking can take away from trusting, genuine conversations.

The book "Drink" by Canadian author and former vice-principal of McGill University, Ann Dousett Johnson was an amazing read and eye opener for me. She writes:

"Our healthcare system is now seeing liver damage in women in their 20s and 30s that they previously only saw in men in their 60s. Women aren't built to metabolize alcohol well as compared to men mainly because we have more body fat than men. Since body fat contains little water, there is less to dilute the alcohol consumed. In addition, women have a lower level of a key metabolizing enzyme, alcohol dehydrogenase, which helps the body break down and eliminate alcohol."

As a Registered Nurse in Acute Care Medicine, Melissa has seen women in their 20s die of liver failure. The damage done is unique to each woman. Melissa says "No one can determine how much, little or how often we drink will affect our body. For women, drinking 2 to 3 drinks (including wine and beer) on average per day can lead to cirrhosis, a condition in which scar tissue replaces healthy liver tissue until the liver cannot function properly."

I am a social drinker and I am very aware that I have unsuccessfully relied on it as a coping mechanism. With my mental health the priority in my life, it was common for me to take 30-60 day breaks from drinking. Those breaks were essential, effective and healthy in my journey. I felt happy, balanced and in control of my life.

I always find that after a night of drinking I feel raw and my anxiety is high. Melissa agrees that being hungover can cause extreme anxiety and it is not fun being there. Nothing feels more powerless than fear and anxiety. Powerlessness is not real, but it definitely feels real in the moment. It could shut my entire system down so mentally and physically I wasn't helpful in any situation.

A few amazing exercises have helped get anxiety under control when it rears its ugly, powerful, forceful head. Once I started to be aware and practice diverting my brain, the less strength that anxiety had. I found that accepting, acknowledging it, not judging myself because of it, letting myself feel and step through the fear, was empowering.

#18. Emergency: Stop Anxiety NOW!

This Mind Trick provides me with a sense of internal power. The steps are easy to grab onto when I'm in a panic and continue to be powerful and when I need to lessen the intensity.

1.   FAB #2: STOP!

2.   BREATHE. Take a deep breath. Then another.
       Go deeper than you think you can go. Do this a
       minimum of 3 times. This can be done several times
       every day. (I was told that taking several deep breaths
       daily can also help you lose weight …)

3.   FAB #9: Feel, See, Hear.

4.   FAB #14: Ground Yourself.

5.   FAB #3: Do. Don't Think.

6.   Take a shower. When I'm feeling overwhelmed and

about to snap, a shower is calming and gives my mind something else to focus on. Showers also stimulate our senses (feel, see, hear, smell) which always distracts me when I'm feeling really overwhelmed.

7.   Do something nice for someone else. Help in the yard or house. Visit a neighbour or friend who you haven't seen for a while.

Get out of your Head and Into the World

"Only a life lived for others is worth living."

- *Albert Einstein*

Volunteering changed me from feeling "mental" to a Mental Health Advocate. When I started to volunteer on a consistent basis, the constant, nagging feeling that I had never done enough in my day disappeared.

The beauty of volunteering is that you benefit as much (if not more) than the people or organization you support. It is amazing the opportunities, friendships and rewards it can bring. Volunteer roles have filled my life with amazing relationships and more work opportunities than either of my college diplomas. When I work hard and overcome difficult situations it makes me feel proud. Feeling proud is an awesome feeling.

Every single one of us has the power to make the world a better place. I would often question if one little Canadian girl could really make an impact? Then I read this quote:

"If you think you are too small to make a difference, try sleeping with a mosquito."

- Dalai Lama

Life can deal some unfair hands but if purpose can be found, the struggle won't consume us. I truly believe that everything we've been through and everything you've learned, no matter how awful, can be used to help others. You are a huge contributor to our earth and the universe's master plan.

I believe that we are built for suffering and if we have life too easy, it can cause mental issues of its own.

Volunteering opened up a beautiful path to my future as well. Working at the Bethany Care Centre for seniors gave me a new respect for our end of days. It also helped me to realize that I wanted to start working with children.

Volunteering at WE Day fills me with purpose and a sense of relief knowing others are dedicated to **changing the world.** Many people and organizations are fighting to ensure all humans on this earth have access to daily basic needs.

Ooooo, and I also got to meet Margaret Trudeau, Jay Shetty, Serena Ryder and Spencer West at various WE Days. I haven't met them yet, but Oprah, Prince Harry and even the Dalai Lama have been speakers!

Volunteering as a literacy tutor and an instructor for the Roots of Empathy program got me the credentials I needed to get a job at the local high school. A job in education was not even close to being on my radar, but the students became some of my most respected life teachers. Working at my local high school is how I met some of my most favourite and supportive women who will be a part of my tribe forever.

Fab Mind Trick

#19. Random Acts of Kindness.

Random acts of kindness (RAK) are so fabulous and are accessible, easy and cheap! They are full of amazing, immeasurable magic and the ripple effect is limitless! They have had the power to make me feel content, worthy and purposeful. A coffee, a nice word, help carrying something, delivering a plant - Google it for some great ideas.[12] I find when I'm looking for opportunities to give Random acts of kindness, they show up at least once a day.

---

[12]https://www.randomactsofkindness.org/the-kindness-blog/2943-50-kindness-ideas-for-random-acts-of-kindness-day

I've talked about being in the moment and recognizing opportunities with my son since he was just a wee babe. We buy for the car behind us at a drive thru, give flowers to neighbours and look for opportunities to be helpful when out and about. I look for ways to RAK at least once everyday and am excited when a chance appears. So when my son was 10 and we were at Theatre Calgary watching the play "Saving Mr. Banks", I was surprised to realize he didn't really know what a RAK was. At intermission, we got in line to get a drink of water from the fountain. Two older women came to the line at the exact same time as us. I said to them, "You two go ahead." In which they replied, "No, no, you two go." We dance around a bit and finally I thanked them and joined the line in front of them. When Jesse and I got to the fountain, I filled a paper cup full of water then turned and offered it to one of the women behind us. I filled a second cup for the ladies; such a small thing, but both women were surprised and grateful for the gesture. As we made our way back to the theatre, my son said "Oh, NOW I get it!" And I asked "Get what?" a little distracted navigating the crowd. "The Random Act of Kindness thing. I never really understood what you had meant before."

Actions speak louder than words. Our kids learn from watching us.

Magical Science

Do you ever feel like you are completely off balance? A feeling that nothing is making sense, you can't find clarity to make the simplest decisions and like all the energy has been sucked out of you by some unknown force?

Throughout my life, beginning in my teens, I have dabbled in energy healing and have experienced first-hand the power of an incredible tool called "Reiki". The energy healing of Reiki has been an outstanding tool for my anxiety and physical wellbeing.

For most Reiki practitioners it's a lifestyle choice and they live by the 5 Reiki principles[13]:
Just for today:

- Just for today, I will not worry
- Just for today, I will not be angry
- Just for today, I will do my work honestly
- Just for today, I will give thanks for my many blessings
- Just for today, I will be kind to my neighbour and every living thing

A Reiki session proved to be equally or more powerful for me than a session with a therapist. And you know I LOVE my therapy! (See "Peace, Love, Therapy" chapter).
If you have never heard of, or tried, Reiki I am here to enlighten you on how Reiki can help sluggish, injured or imbalanced-feeling people feel more energetic and clear-headed.

I was feeling very unbalanced one night when a Facebook post from my now life-long friend, Sandy Maloy popped up proud and beautiful and got my attention. Sandy was born and raised

---

[13] sacredwellness.co/the-five-reiki-principles/

in my town and is a gift to this earth. She genuinely cares about the physical and mental health of all souls on this planet.

A picture of Sandy and the following copy filled my screen:

"Hi! I'm Sandy and I am a Karuna Reiki Master, Raindrop Therapist, Holistic Healer, Bamboo Massage, Chakra Balancing, Plant Based Nutritionist, Herbalist, Soundbath Facilitator. My journey began in Plant Based Nutrition, which in turn introduced me to Essential Oils and Raindrop Therapy. I am a Usui Reiki Master and have a studio where I do many types of energy healing combined with massage. I am certified with Hot Stone, Myofascial Cupping, Crystal Healing and am on my way in acquiring my Master Herbalist Certification. I also am a CanFit Pro certified Personal Trainer and Fitness Instructor. I love helping people and my goal is to find natural health solutions to enhance quality of life, prevent and reverse illness, and help you feel the best you can body, mind and soul!"

Sandy didn't hesitate when I asked her to share a few of her stories for this book. Her gifts, passion and knowledge are a rare find, and I truly can't express how completely excited I am to be able to share her with you!

For our book interview, we decided to go thrift store shopping and have a vegan lunch date. Sandy started to educate me about the history of Reiki. It was started by a christian minister and professor at a university in Japan, Dr. Mikao Usui. Usui started research on why miracles happen. During this time, he discovered that Jesus, the apostles, Buddha and many other famous teachers and leaders all over the world were practicing hands on healing techniques which seemed to result in MIRACLES.

Dr. Usui spent his life doing this research and gave the techniques and teachings he discovered the name "Reiki"[14].

With so much to discover about energy healing, I won't go into the whole shabang, but I can tell you, IT WORKS! There are many people who have discovered Reiki and dedicate their lives to helping others clear their energy blocks so they can function daily feeling balanced, clear, evolved and at peace.

When I met Sandy about six years ago, she wasn't yet a Reiki Master. She was offering her clients massage treatments including raindrop and hot stone, but she was sending clients interested in Reiki to another practitioner. Clients were asking her about Reiki more frequently, so she finally decided to go for her first treatment. Being a whole-hearted healer, Sandy went to experience it so she could educate herself and share it with confidence to her clients. At the time, Sandy didn't feel that her life was suffering in any way that she needed Reiki healing.

---

[14] reiki.org

WELL, her very first Reiki session was LIFE CHANGING. She told me over vegan burrito bowls, "I felt like a whole new

person. I didn't realize I could feel that good. She specifically remembers a memory that came up where she could physically feel herself sitting on her grandfather's lap and could hear his heartbeat. "It was magical for me."

A Reiki treatment begins with you laying down and getting very comfortable. You focus on how your body feels and where tension is felt. Many times, the practitioner doesn't even touch you. In my sessions with Sandy, she will sometimes talk me through a guided journey. Mentally she will take me to an amazing place, discover what is causing me unnecessary hardship and then we leave it behind. It has been so amazing to experience.

QIGONG (Chi-gong)

Sandy then introduced me to Qigong (a more medical and deliberate form of Reiki), and it blew my mind! Qigong is estimated to be over 4,000 years old and has been used for centuries for healing in China. The therapy is based on the traditional Chinese belief that the human body contains a network of energy pathways through which vital energy, called Qi (also called chi or vital energy) circulates. It supports the energy in our bodies to flow freely. Qigong is used in integrative medicine to complement or supplement accepted medical treatments, including relaxation, physical health, rehabilitation and treatment of specific diseases.

In the 1900s, China wanted to ban Qigong or any healing methods (like acupuncture) that hadn't been scientifically proven. To be allowed to be used in Chinese hospitals, the

Chinese government assigned several accredited scientists, under strict conditions, to provide proof that the practice

actually worked. Studies were conducted within China as well as other countries and the experiments conclusively showed the practice of Qigong enabled many patients to recover from their diseases.

It was SCIENTIFICALLY PROVEN that energy work HEALS OUR BODIES. It has been used for centuries in other parts of the world (mainly in Asia) and now, with access to the internet, the rest of the world has been able to learn this healing method.

Note: *If you are sceptical, Google: The eight circuits of the brain*

Our Chakras

A chakra is a spinning wheel of energy. If you could see your body and it's frequency, the energy all flows in a circular orbit. If we could make all of our microscopic atoms and molecules visible, your atoms would be away from your nucleus by 25 miles.

Science has proven our bodies are made up of 7 chakras. And when they are blocked, our bodies don't function as productively.[15]

---

[15] gostica.com/aura-science/proof-energy-chakras-confirmed-science-finally-proves-meridians-exist/

Fab Mind Trick

#20. Balance Your Chakras.

When I started with energy healing, I didn't know what my chakras were, how they worked, that they could even be blocked and that working with them is actually a viable and effective treatment option for many things including: stress relief, depression, low energy levels and chronic pain.

There are many believers and I am one of them: life is made easier with the chakras balanced and fully functioning.

I've just recently learned that our chakras play a huge part in our mental wellbeing. Think how: **every tiny trauma we go through can defines how we live, grow and learn. It is very easy to get stuck there, in the confusion and pain and sadness.**

When my chakras are balanced, my body feels lighter and my head is clear. I feel like I've just taken the best nap ever!

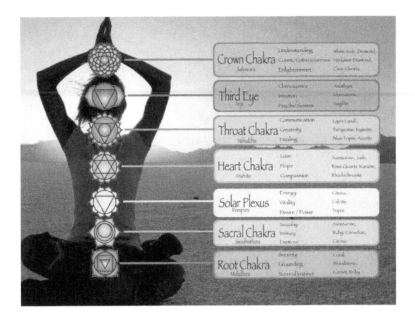

Our chakras can affect our physical body as well. They physically work with the endocrine system in our body and join with the secondary chakra. So each chakra, if blocked, (for example solar plexus chakra and hips) can cause sensations and injuries in parts of our body.

The law of attraction in quantum physics proves that lower vibrations are attracted to lower vibrations and visa-versa. Positive, healthy people often surround themselves with like-minded people because that's who they attract. When our chakras are open and flowing, we are vibrating on a higher frequency. If your chakras are blocked, you are vibrating at a lower frequency.

High frequency chakras can mean prosperity, abundance and success in your work and relationships. Open, balanced chakras will attract others who are functioning optimally as well.

Each chakra has its job/function. Here are a few examples:

Sacral chakra. Holds guilt, social conditioning. What we are told to believe is right or wrong.

Crown chakra. Responsible for our ego.

Root chakra. Helps us feel grounded, comfortable and that we belong. Sensations of knowing you are allowed (shall I venture - entitled) to be you and appreciate what you have in your life. To feel abundance. This helps fears and anxieties and worries get blocked.

When I had my Root Chakra cleared and balanced, I noticed that I was able to recognize the emotions that I was feeling, acknowledge why and address them. Then they were gone. Negative feelings, guilt and shame I'd had for years were just gone!

When I leave a Reiki/Chakra session, I feel about 30 pounds lighter than before I walked in. The process of clearing my chakras has enabled me to find and live in my truth which has been outstanding. Finding my truth before wasn't an option because I was too confused and overwhelmed - trapped in my abusive relationship with myself.

Years and years of negative feelings and self talk haven't completely disappeared so I choose to invest time and money in energy healing every 6-8 weeks. It is an investment in my mental health and I know it pays off by making my life more peaceful. Dealing with present and past challenges is easier. It's magical SCIENCE that WORKS!

Energy Healing for Grief

I knew I had been holding on to the loss of my second (and last) pregnancy. When we lose someone we love and they are a part of our hearts, the intense grief can block the positive flow of one or several chakras. For a woman, the loss of a child at any stage of growth creates catastrophic emotional and physical obstacles.

I believe the hardships we endure in life exist so that, one day, when someone we Love more than ourselves is struggling, we can not only listen but truly and completely understand.

We all experience loss and the resulting anxiety. We can learn how to identify what we are feeling, work with it and heal from it. Grief can weave itself into every single fibre of our being so it can take a commitment. I think it is important to know that we are entitled to feel sad, but if grief is allowed to take over our lives, it can be a long life of suffering.

Understanding and working with my chakra system has given me a new perspective on compassion. I began to come from a different state of awareness when in situations with others who are fundamentally different than I am. This felt amazing, enlightening and aligned with my no judgement practice as well.

An outstanding story that Sandy shared with me:

"I had a client that was EXTREMELY racist. I was surprised when they came to me for Reiki because I didn't know how it would go. To me, I always thought of racism as hatred. When I was working with them, specifically their root chakra, the amount of fear they were holding had the chakra completely blocked. This person believed many things they had heard as a child, for example, "Muslims are going to take over the world and enforce their laws on everyone." They were sucked into this fear, completely believing that it could happen. Hatred wasn't the driving force, intense fear was. Understanding that their feelings were fear-driven gave me the compassion to work with them instead of sitting there in complete disagreement."

If you are wanting to get yourself to a place of peace and understanding about yourself, I highly recommend learning about energy healing and your chakras. Get to know them. Learn how to work with and understand them. When you understand yourself better, it makes it easier to interact with other people in your life.

"Energy healing is so important that I think if they taught level 1 Reiki in school, as a mandatory subject, we would solve almost all of the world's problems." Sandy believes this with her whole heart.

Solve our world's problems? Imagine!!

You Have all you Need.

When searching for a way to incorporate an exercise routine (healthy body, healthy mind) into my life, I found Kundalini yoga. Really, it found me and it had a HUGE impact.

While writing this book, I've realized amazing things find us when we are paying attention and open to them.

I picked the Kundalini class only because the location was amazing, it seemed low impact and the time worked for me. I was looking for something to relax me, not anything high impact. I loved Kundalini yoga instantly because I found it to be more of a mental exercise than physical. If you know the reality tv show 'Survivor', envision the challenges. To win depends on mental strength. Also, In every class that I went to, I would have at least one AH-HA moment. I was amazed to discover that short, simple mental or physical exercises can have a profound effect in creating mental wellness.

At the end of one class our beautiful instructor, Stef, told us this:

"Everything is already within you. You have all you need, exactly what you need is right inside of you."

Those words knocked me to another mind set and it felt amazing. After a Friday class, I asked Stef if she would be interested in having tea one day to talk about the book I was writing. I wanted to dive into her perspective on the importance of mental and physical exercise. Stef is also a chiropractor and I was intrigued by her combination of skills.

A week later, Stef and I met at her house. While we sat on the floor drinking tea, watching her (super cute) two year old play with the two dogs, Stef shared her philosophies with me.

Stef is a huge advocate in all of us realizing our power. When something in life is out of our control, she feels it is imperative to work through the issue and not dwell on it for too long. "Life gives hard times to us all. Sometimes it sucks huge. Let yourself feel it and then let go of everything that isn't serving you anymore." This is not easy for me to do so I get help.

"One exercise takes 3 minutes." she said as she lifted her arms up in the air in a "V" shape. "It sounds simple, but it is a struggle. A struggle that only you can go through. That 3 minutes is really hard! You have to really focus on your inner strength to get through it. And when you do, there is an ecstasy that you feel afterwards."

Stef shared her admiration for Dr. John Demartini and a quote from a speech she heard him deliver.

"Do you want to be a victim of your past, or the master of your destiny? And this is up to you."

For Stef, Kundalini yoga is instrumental in helping others get out of the past and the victim mindset it can cause. Specifically, the teachings of Yogi Bhajan inspired her.

"Yogi Bhajan taught me that when we are in a low state of mind, which he calls "cold depression", people are sad and confused and anxious but they don't know why. I could relate so I took some time to learn about him."

Born Harbhajan Singh Puri, August 26, 1929, in the part of India that became Pakistan in 1948, he was the son of a medical doctor, attended a Catholic convent school and he spent his youth in privileged environments (private schools and summers at the exclusive Dalhousie mountain region of Himachal Pradesh).

When he was just eight years old he began his yogic training with an enlightened teacher, Sant Hazara Singh, who proclaimed Yogi to be a Master of Kundalini Yoga when he was sixteen and a half.

In September of 1968, he left India for Canada to teach yoga at Toronto University, carrying a letter of recommendation from Sir James George, Canadian High Commissioner in New Delhi, who had been his student. After two months in Canada, he flew to Los Angeles for a weekend visit where he met a number of young hippies, the spiritual seekers of that era. Yogi immediately recognized that the experience of higher consciousness they were attempting to find through drugs could be achieved by practicing the science of Kundalini Yoga, as well as rebuilding their nervous systems.[16]

Stef credits Kundalini yoga for getting her out of the victim mindset. "It's all good to talk about but not as easy to do. For instance, if I feel I need to be more loving to myself or open

---

[16] yogibhajan.org The Kundalini Research Institute 2009.

my heart centre, I can talk about what that might mean, but Kundalini not only identified that cognition, it gave me an action that I can do myself".

Echoing what Stef said, Kundalini gave me tangible things that I can work on myself. I don't have to go anywhere. I just have to show up, commit, and have the discipline to do it consistently.

"Us, YOU, who we are, it starts with our beliefs. More specifically, limiting beliefs. A lot of those beliefs come from subconscious downloads from our childhood." Stef believes that it is essential for us to tap into the conscious and unconscious mind when working through an emotional issue. "We may never find out exactly where our thoughts or behaviours originated from and at some point, it doesn't matter anymore."

Stef also believes that it is important for parents and caregivers to understand the human brain development starting at birth. She explains: *"As children, we are in straight download mode until about age 7. We are not really conscious of our actions or what we are doing in our environment (to an extent), we are just downloading everything into our subconscious mind. The subconscious mind is what drives our thoughts."*

Our thoughts drive our behaviour, which drive our actions, which drive our results and beliefs. It's a vicious cycle."

Stef suggests TRIAGING YOUR LIMITING BELIEFS. Prioritize. Decide what is the worst of them and start knocking them off one by one.

Pay attention to see what emotional state you are in most of the time. Assess your current state of beliefs and identify your limiting beliefs. Then identify what your IDEAL self is. Compare it to your actual self. In the work she has done, most people at this stage will have an automatic thought that comes to surface and the majority of the time it is negative. The negative ones are fast and sneaky and they are NOT TRUE.

The worst part is that we can completely BELIEVE it. They then become part of who we are.

When Stef graduated from chiropractic school, she was $250,000 in debt. She married a chiropractor so they were $500,000 in debt. An automatic thought she could easily have had is, *"I will never be out of debt."* She decided to look at the evidence for and against that thought. *"I work hard and I'm making money",* for example.

She reframed her cognitive awareness around it: "Even though I have a lot of debt, that debt allowed me to do what I'm doing now. I work hard to be able to pay that money back. Yes I'm in debt. But that money was money that I used to get an education with. I'm working hard now while I repay it and I'm also helping people".

As she told me the story, I could physically feel the weight of a $250,000 debt and then the more significant $500,000. When the thought was reframed, I could feel that weight lift. By recognizing and changing the dialog, it helps our mental and physical body.

My point here is that you can mentally and physically improve yourself with non-invasive exercises. Start with something small, simple and you have a bit of an interest in. To meet your needs where you are right now.

The exercise part is not about losing weight (cool if it happens), but a way to feel **proud of yourself. Only YOU can do it.** When it comes to our physical body, only we, the individual can put in the effort. Only you make it happen and get 100% of the credit.

Physical challenges help us express emotions, feel strong, force us to be in the moment, make us breathe better, impress ourselves.

Mentally acknowledge the small successes to yourself. Acknowledge every and any small step.

#21. Breathe and Exercise in Nature.

Earth cure me. Earth receive my woe.
Rock strengthen me. Rock receive my weakness.
Rain wash my sadness away. Rain receive my doubt.
Sun make sweet my song. Sun receive the anger from my heart.
- Nancy Wood. Earth Prayers from Around the World.

Breath not only keeps us alive, it is a powerful healing tool. I started taking conscious deep breaths 3-5 times a day when I read that it can help us lose weight! I can't say that has happened but I did notice an increase in patience and energy.

I haven't written about exercise much but there is no doubt that getting the heart rate up at least once a day is good for our mental health. I try not to make it about weight, just overall health. When I have made getting a sweat on a priority, my days are calmer and happier.

Getting outside and fresh air 98.4% of the time activates my creative brain and brings me clarity.

5. The New Relationship

"Happiness is a fickle creature. A constant companion to some, hides herself completely from others. She's been an elusive creature to me. But, here she is, finally, sitting among us, and I say welcome. I won't mention how late her arrival is."

- Princess Margaret in Season 3 of The Crown.

When I started to be aware and focusing on discovering who I truly am and born to be, the fog started to lift. When I began to honour and trust my unique personality, I became more confident and let myself be more adventurous.

As a mental health advocate, trying to figure out why I was abusive to myself for so long (and still can be) has been difficult. It's a huge soup pot with various ingredients from each chapter of my life - there isn't one specific thing that I can pinpoint. How much is nature vs nurture or genetics vs experience? What I know for sure, is that you need YOU! Only you can create the life you want for yourself.

I had to find a way to love myself, be proud of myself, trust my thoughts, words, actions. I believe it was having my one and only baby is what triggered my abusive brain to emerge full force. But the beautiful thing is it motivated me to become the best version of myself. I needed to find a way to create a solid, consistent roos system to support and nourish myself and for my family.

Targeting the most harmful patterns/thoughts first, being aware of how often they are happening and then choosing weapons from a kit larger and more amazing than I could have ever dreamed (there are endless resources. So many beautiful people dedicated to helping each one of us heal and start running with the positive energy flow) has ultimately shifted the way my brain thinks, the language it uses and how it processes information.

The practice of being in the moment and stopping negative thoughts as soon as I'm aware of them has rewired my brain and an incredible shift happened. When the shift happens, you will know it. Time always (or mostly) seems to be on my side, patience is there when I need it, ideas and inspiration are constant, and you notice the small miracles in life.

When I put other people first, I put my problems on the back burner (very sure a diversion technique!). I had to experience some raw awareness, real conversations, therapy sessions and soberness until I figured out why I was struggling so much.

When I tried to find a few things I found joy in, I truly didn't know what I liked - what I liked to do, what soda to drink, how to dress ...etc. On advice from a therapist, I asked others who knew me to notice when I would light up talking about a certain topic. It took some time to find out what true success meant to me. I realized that what I wanted didn't fit my core belief of what my perception/idea of being productive was.

Instead of beating myself up for walking (instead of running or something more vigorous), reading, lunching, movies, cuddling on the couch, I focus on all the gifts in my life that I am grateful for. Instead of feeling overwhelmed by selfishness for my first-world problems, I trained my brain to only focus on what I'm so lucky to have.

Changing even the smallest things has created huge transformation.

I tattooed the word "trust" on my wrist and look at it daily, letting that word turn into a feeling to wrap around my whole body. I let myself imagine what it felt like to be ok with constantly growing and evolving and changing. I gave myself permission to choose different hobbies, interests, groups, foods. I tried not to have so many rules for myself. I let my days be led by what felt right (not at all easy) instead of the "shoulds". I reminded myself that I am an awesome "Late Bloomer" and I didn't have to be in Love with a hobby so much that I'd become an expert or go to the Olympics or buy a business or choose a life-long career. I just had to try it.

The mantra, "do, don't think" became a solid rock. I woke up every morning and zipped myself up and tried to smile and be kind to everything and everybody: my house, neighbourhood, community, social media, my closest Luvs, myself. I walked with a playlist with songs like Sarah McLachlan's "Angel", Pink's "Perfect" and Ben Folds Five "Cooler Than me". They helped me feel understood. I had Sarah's lyrics from "Ordinary Miracle" printed on my wall so I could see them everyday and wire my brain to KNOW that life is a gift every single day:

"Life is like a gift, they say,
wrapped up for you every day."

– Sarah McLachlan

I did, and still do, all of the FABulous Mind Tricks. If our brain can create the issues, then it also has the power completely to undo them. It's our brain that is causing the stress so it can stop the stress, too.

The brain is imagining the negative outcomes, therefore it can just as easily imagine positive ones.

Know and BELIEVE that every single experience that got you here will serve you at some point. TRUST that you are learning for someone you will desperately want to help at some point and the only way to do that is to understand. Not try to understand, but fully, completely understand because you have been in the exact same place. You have experienced it.

Rough times can lead to huge, awesome change or light a fire under our butts. Bad choices can lead us to some amazing experiences and people and teach us how to evolve.

You can do lots of things, but you can't do everything at once. Be patient. Pick a few and make them your priority.

Believe that there is a solution to every problem. Finding out EXACTLY what the problem is might not be easy and could take time. Help! Get help!!

I had a big problem I couldn't solve. I couldn't seem to physically start typing out this book. I had written notes in several notebooks, made voice clips on several devices, sent texts and emails, images of quotes and inspirational sayings to myself. So much was going on in my head. How could I possibly organize it all? It took someone from my Tribe (Lyndsie, you complete me!) to give me a deadline and light a fire under my butt. Having someone believe in me and work beside me has been essential to the process.

92% of people don't achieve their goals. Why?
They can't take the first step or recognize the barricades.[17]

To write this book, I almost had to become a different person. I had to stop procrastinating. I Love books and I am a reader. Historical fiction is always my go-to, so writing a self-help book was completely out of my element!

I had to choose to put down Candy Crush (Love it. It's so colourful and fun and beating the levels makes me happy and I'm sticking to the story that it helps keep my brain healthy!) I had to stop Googling the "British Royals" and decide to binge

---

[17] forbes.com

watch "Queer Eye" after I got some work done. I knew it was going to be a lot of work. I needed to start - but I wasn't starting. Instead of getting down on myself about it (working on shifting the negative narrative as soon as it starts), I tried to observe, understand and find a solution. It took a long time. Months. Writing a book is a dream come true for me, but back then, it was looming over me like a dark cloud. It was causing me to not want to get out of bed because the task seemed too enormous. I knew I could do it if only I would just start! But I also knew I was standing in my own way and didn't know why.

It amazes me how easy it was to make the struggle invisible. Someone can be completely at war on the inside, but appear to the outside world like they are functioning just fine. Through this daily struggle of a journey, I know that if we choose, we can train our brain to consistently be supportive and notice the positives. With tons of patience, humour, trust, kindness and the practice of focusing on solutions, the positive thoughts will start to automatically trump the negative before they can begin. It has worked for me.

If you are in an abusive relationship with yourself, I wish for you that my story will help you get out. Find out what is causing the abuse and FAB Mind Trick the crap out of them! One day (of course when you least expect it), you will be hit with the powerful realization that the hard work has paid off and you have evolved. You will look calm on the outside, but also be calm on the inside.

I can type this without one hesitation, my autopilot mode is now 90% positive. I don't seek sleep and solitude nearly as much. I do find days can still be a bit frantic, but I'm not constantly feeling overwhelmed and exhausted. I am patient, having fun in the moment and creating new dreams.

Sparkle with who you are! It inspires and liberates others to do the same.

Thank you, fabulous reader, for reading my words. You are magical. We are magical. Life can be magical.

If you are interested in digging deeper into the process of rewiring your brain, sign up for my next workshop at careywilkinsonlee.com.

Sources

1. chopracentermeditation.com - **Page 29**

2. tarataylor.com - **Page 32**

3. pediaa.com/difference-between-perception-and-perspective - Page 34

4. thelawofattraction.com/learn-trust-intuition - **Page 41**

5. rootsofempathy.org - **Page 53**

6. verywellmind.com/what-is-locus-of-control-2795434 - Page 56

7. 21-day Mediation Experience: chopracentermeditation.com - Page 63

8. The Center for Addiction & Mental Health: camh.ca - Page 71

9. The Emotion Wheel: What It Is and How To Use It: positivepsychology.com - **Page 80**

10. Book: Your Child is A Person by Alexander Thomas, Stella Chess & Herbert G. Birch - Page 85

11. academia.edu and healthofchildren.com/T/Temperament - Page 86

12. randomactsofkindness.org - **Page 103**

13. sacredwellness.co/the-five-reiki-principles - **Page 105**

14. reiki.com - **Page 107**

15. gostica.com/aura-science/proof-energy-chakras-confirmed-science-finally-proves-meridians-exist - **Page 109**

16. yogibhajan.org - **Page 116**

17. forbes.com/sites/dandiamond/2013/01/01/just-8-of-people-achieve-their-new-years-resolutions-heres-how-they-did-it/#498d2ab3596b - **Page 124**

FAB Mind Tricks Guide

#1. Negative to Positive. Page 22

This mind trick was LIFE-CHANGING! Bringing awareness to and catching all of the negative narrative without a judgemental eye, gave me a running start to healing. It had such a positive impact and gave me the confidence I needed to know I was going to be free of my abusive thoughts.

#2. STOP! Page 27

Just STOP. Catch the thought as soon as you become aware of it. Visualizing a huge stop sign works for me. Stop the thought, take 3 super huge deep breaths and then tell yourself something positive. If you are remembering a moment in the past that you are reliving and feeling regret about, STOP, breath and say something like, "I am doing the best I can. I am learning and making informed choices." I still depend on this trick daily, but I am catching the thoughts way faster - before they have a chance to affect my physical and mental space is my goal.

#3. Do. Don't Think. Page 28

Start doing something. Anything to distract you.

- Colour, draw, write, do push ups, call a friend, write a letter.
- Focus on getting ready and go for a walk (FAB Trick #15. Feel, See, Hear to get grounded), take some pictures. Look for the ordinary miracles that surround you.

- Make dinner, sing, dance, play with the dog/kids, organize the basement or garage. Do a Negative to Positive list!

Take a shower. When I'm feeling overwhelmed and about to snap, a shower is calming and gives my mind something else to focus on. Showers also stimulate our senses (feel, see, hear, smell) which always helps me feel grounded.

#4. Balance your Ego. Page 31

When I started, I balanced my ego two times a day, once in the morning and once at night. I found that the effects were almost instant. When functioning from my higher self, my emotions don't affect me physically. My mind is more decisive and I am able to listen to and trust my instincts.
I have been balancing my ego everyday for over 10 years. It's very little effort for a huge result (in my opinion). It can be done anytime, anywhere, several times a day.

- Take 3 deep breaths.

- Say in your head or out loud "Today I come from my higher self and I balance my ego."

- Repeat at least 7 times. I keep saying it until I feel that my body is responding to the message (I feel a shift in my consciousness and awareness). The goal is to be balanced and make decisions today from that place.

- End with "This is my truth."

#5. Positive Affirmations. Page 35

Any Saturday Night Live fans in the house? The Stuart Smalley skits and his daily affirmations were one of my favourites. They made me laugh but also introduced me to the power of positive affirmations. Ironic and fabulous that SNL gave me this one. I have used them consistently when the negative brain tries to over power the positive.

Works best if done at least once daily. But not limited to just once.

Take 3 deep breaths and read your Positive Affirmations out loud:

Today I trust that I am exactly where I am meant to be. Don't forget the infinite possibilities that you were born with. I wish you contentment with who you are and that you use and share your unique gifts in this world.

- To get more Love, I simply have to Love myself more
- I allow myself to think big dreams
- I attract only good things in my life
- I am a unique individual with my own path to follow
- I am courageous and brave
- I like the way I look
- I am powerful
- I am a good sleeper
- I am beautiful inside and out
- I am safe. In my house, in my town, in my world
- I am a fast learner
- I have lots of great ideas. I am very creative
- I am a good influence on others
- I deserve good things
- I recognize all of the gifts in my life. I focus on the positive
- I can do anything I set my mind to. My dreams are coming true

Customize your Positive Affirmations list, print it and put where you can see it daily. Make more than one if you want.

#6. Talk to Your Angels. Page 39

I believe in angels. I believe that we are born with them around us. They stay close and are there waiting for the second we need them. When I am feeling lost, scared, worried about my family or the future or at a point where I am feeling helpless, I talk to them. First, I always thank them for everything they do that I don't see. Then I wish, tell, ask, cry and pray. I can feel that I am being heard. My body shifts to a place of peace and relief and I feel, without a doubt, that I am not alone. We are never alone. Our angels are guarding over us, instantly ready to help.

#7. Don't Watch the News. Page 40

When we would watch the evening news, my dad would tell me, "If it doesn't bleed, it doesn't lead." This meant that the news usually focuses on "bleed" or shocking, terrible stories. For an empath, this can have an instant, negative effect (especially at night before bed). I also stay away from shows and movies about abuse, abductions, killers, cruelty to animals. I'm not saying to not be aware of how we can make our world a better place. But hearing and seeing stories about evil and we can't do anything to change or stop it can be extremely overwhelming.

#8. Zip Yourself Up. Page 43

This beauty goes way back. I found it worked instantly and I Love it because it lets me stay in bed a bit longer. I did it every morning for months and I pull it out when lacking confidence or inspiration.

Essentially, this is a "fake it until you make it" exercise. It is a visualization that has you zipping yourself up in a whole new body. The body of the person you want to be. It helped me to get into a mental state where I felt like I could conquer the day ahead.

- Start at your toes. What do they look like? Mine are always super cute. My feet? Like I just had a pedicure yesterday.
- I make myself a little taller - my legs are longer (as well as hairless and completely smooth).
- In my zip up visualization, I don't have any knee pain and I am dressed in a comfy yet very stylish outfit.

Move up your entire body, visualizing how you want to feel and present yourself to the world that day. For me, I am feeling decisive, adventurous and excited to find out what the day ahead of me has to offer. My zipped up version of myself is a confident, competent mom who is grateful for the little things and recognizes the gifts that life has to offer. She is laughing, has a quick wit and is mentally prepared for the battle of another day.

Zip yourself up every morning. And in between if you want to.

#9. Feel, See, Hear. Page 50

To get yourself grounded and your brain focused on the present moment.
- Stop what you are doing and focus on your body and your surroundings.
- What are 3 things you can feel? Your toes in your shoes. Air coming through your nostrils, wind on your face.
- Then focus on things you can see. A tree, bird, your hands in your lap.
- Then focus on things you can hear. A tv on, creaks of the house, a dog barking, traffic, kids playing, the wind in the trees.

There is no limit to how many things you choose to feel, see and hear or often or how long you do it. I find it works every time and has been my #1 go-to for bringing me into the present.

#10. Tribe. Page 54

Spend time with your people, your tribe. Like-minded friends that see, respect, and get you. Your tribe is filled with those who know that you are human and aren't perfect but Love you and laugh with you anyway. You've been through the ugly together and you're still in. Those who on your team even when you are not in the room (got your back, don't talk behind it). These are people (or pets) in your life that are your tribe. What I have learned, it is NEVER TOO LATE to join, create and be a part of a tribe. As we evolve, our relationships evolve. Find a new tribe if you need one. Nourish your tribe relationships.

Volunteer at a community event or join a group or a class. Pay attention to events going on around you and that catch your attention. Trust your gut, follow a spark and meet your people. Quality, not quantity.

"Love grows brains!"
 - Roots of Empathy Program

#11. "I am Magic". Page 59

A word that describes how I want to feel everyday is MAGICAL.

With this trick, I use the word magical, but pick any word that resonates with you.

- Pick the word for you. Say to yourself, (saying it out loud is powerful): "I am MAGICAL!" I'll say my name sometimes for an even greater impact (even writing this is making me smile a little because I feel a bit silly but it works). "Carey, you are magical! Today I'm going to be magical, feel magical and scatter beautiful magic to others I meet!"
- Say it again and pay attention to how your body feels.
- Repeat as many times as you want and to feel the word has made an impact.

This is a trick I still use daily because I can physically FEEL my body change. Each cell seems to adjust to the Love and possibility of being magical!

Note: I sometimes took it deeper:
"I am magical. And everything that I am going through right now and everything I have experienced and done in my past, the way my brain works, the way I've grown up, ALL of these experiences are helping me to be the person I need to be to help the people I Love the most. I am magical and my unique experience makes me the perfect person to help others navigate their lives while on this earth. To help them live, create, find purpose, live adventurous, content lives and realize their amazing, unique gifts."

#12. Squeeze and Release. Page 66

- Start at your toes and squeeze them, crunch them up.
- Hold for a few breaths and then release.
  Then point your toes and do the same. Hold, breath and release.
- Work your way up the whole body. Make a fist, hold, release, tighten your ab muscles, hold, release. I squeeze my butt cheeks together and squish up my face too.

There aren't any rules. Where is your body feeling stress? The idea is to release any tension, distract the mind and hopefully exhaust the body and relax enough to fall asleep.

#13. Clear your Energy. Page 70

Use this anytime you are feeling anxious. I often use this one before socializing in big groups, when feeling stressed while driving and whenever I am feeling overwhelmed. Can do sitting or standing.

- Take 3 deep breaths.
- With your flat palm facing your body, put your right palm up by your left shoulder.
- Swipe up and down rapidly the length of your whole torso, while taking quick exhales of breaths with each swipe. Do the same thing on the opposite side. After doing the torso, you can do both arms, legs, back - whole body if you want.

If you are feeling negative energy from someone specific or feeling you are attaching emotions to someone that isn't serving you in your life, you can imagine the breaking of the joined energy while doing this.

#14. Ground Yourself. Page 76

A beautiful friend, Sandy introduced me to one of the best grounding experiences I've ever had. We are pulling on the strength from our earth and the energy from our sky.
- Lay down and get extremely comfortable.
- Close your eyes, put your arms to your sides and turn your palms to face the earth.
- Take 3 deep, cleansing (imagine pulling in the positive and breathing out all negative) breaths.
- The next inhale, imagine pulling in all of the love and strength from our earth (Mother Earth). Feel the solid strength fill you.
- On your exhale, pull in the light, energy and healing properties from our powerful sky and sunshine.

- Repeat this until you feel you have cleared your negative thoughts and feelings and are now filled up with a solid foundation and the positive energy.
- Then I imagine clean, healing water coming down on me. All over, around and through me. As it passes through, I visualize it takes all of the toxins, grief, guilt, shame, regret (anything you don't feel is serving you anymore) with it.

#15. A Good Cry. Page 84

When I'm having a hard time understanding what my emotions are trying to tell me, I can feel extremely overwhelmed and stressed. I highly recommend a long, hard & ugly cry. No matter who you are, I whole-heartedly believe a good cry can be extremely helpful for our body to let go of tension. The goal is to feel lighter, clear headed, free!

If it starts on its own, just let it happen for as long as it lasts. If starting to cry doesn't come easily, which doesn't for me (and I'm a crier), a movie can get me started. Have you ever seen the movie, "My Life" with Nicole Kidman and Michael Keaton?

When I have been feeling stress for several days and I can't shake it, I'll plan for a time when I know I'll be in my own space and alone. I Love having my favourite snacks, putting on my most comfy clothes and picking the movie. I make sure I have at least one box of Kleenex close by.

While you are crying, think of things that are making you sad or causing you grief. Let yourself dig deep and feel it all. Cry harder. Visit regrets and heartbreak and the stress you have about money, raising a good kid, what the future will hold. Feel the pain and sadness through your whole body. Don't resist or try to stop - once you are in, take full advantage and heal. Curl in a ball, walk around, lie on the floor or bed - there are no rules. You will know when you are finished. Take deep breaths, sleep, bust out your awesome dance playlist and dance, clean the house, go for a walk, finish the movie - whatever feels right for you.

Note: Other movies that always worked for me: Dead Poets Society, ET, Steel Magnolias, Benji (any movie separating a dog and it's owner will do it). A music "Cry Playlist" can also do the trick. Songs that remind you of someone, the past, what you let slip away (friends, relationships, opportunities …). Again, be alone so you can be long & loud.

#16. Gratitude. Page 89

This trick is a treasure and high on the 'Secret to Life' list. In my opinion, gratitude is significant to healing and will pay its weight in pure gold. It is an essential piece. Stopping the negative dialog and only noticing everything I can think of to be grateful for in my day/life has had outstanding effects. I know that some days, it can be hard to be grateful for anything. What I know, there is ALWAYS something to be grateful for. I have found hundreds in a day! For this trick, focus on the tiny things countless times a day.

- I can wiggle my toes. And they don't hurt!
- Cold water AND hot water. At the same source and each tap in my house can do this!
- A loving pet
- A toaster that toasts
- Rain to feed the plants
- Eye sight, hearing, tastebuds
- Your favourite pjs, a chai latte, a green light
- A motivational talking, Mr. Rogers trinket

The possibilities are endless. Being grateful for the small things has been an amazing tool for me.

#17. Have Fun with Menial Tasks. Page 17

Doing daily, necessary menial tasks is the perfect time to
practice being in the moment and recognizing things to be
grateful for. Find a way to make them fun.
It is so easy for our minds to focus on the negative when doing
chores (even that word makes some cringe). When you sing,
play music, make a game of it, the time seems to go by faster. I
feel that when we are in the moment, doing your best job at
your menial tasks (cleaning, cooking, shovelling, homework …)
being happy while doing it can't hurt, so what do you have to
lose? And if you have a child watching? You are setting them up
for a life of positive and fun in the everyday.

I Love to think of John Lennon's lyrics from the song
"Beautiful Boy. "Life is what happens to you while you are busy
making other plans." I truly believe that if you keep a positive
attitude and always do your best job, opportunities will come to
you when you least expect it!

#18. Emergency! Stop Anxiety NOW! Page 100

This Mind Trick has been tested countless times by me. It
provides me with a sense of internal power and I was able, over
time, to harness it. The steps are easy to grab onto when I'm in
a panic and proved to be powerful and lessen the intensity.

1.   STOP! FAB #2

2.   BREATHE. Take a deep breath. Then another.
        Go deeper than you think you can go. Do this a
        minimum of 3 times. This can be done several times
        every day. (I was told that taking several deep breaths
        daily can also help you lose weight …)

3.   Feel, See, Hear. FAB #9

4.   Ground Yourself. FAB #14

5.   Do. Don't Think. FAB #3

6.   Take a shower. When I'm feeling overwhelmed and about to snap, a shower is calming and gives my mind something else to focus on. Showers also stimulate our senses (feel, see, hear, smell) which always distracts me when I'm feeling really overwhelmed.

7.   Do something nice for someone else. Help in the yard or house. Visit a neighbour or friend who you haven't seen for a while.

#19. Random Acts of Kindness. Page 103

Random acts of kindness are so fabulous and they are accessible, easy and cheap! They are full of amazing, immeasurable magic and the ripple effect is limitless! They are so easy and free and they have had the power to make me feel content, worthy and purposeful. A coffee, a nice word, help carrying something, deliver a plant - google it for some great ideas. … They can be tiny or day (week, month, life) changing. I find when I'm looking for opportunities everyday, they show up.

#20. Balance your Chakras. Page 110

When I started with energy healing, I didn't know what my chakras were, how they worked, that they could even be blocked and that working with them is actually a viable and effective treatment option for many things including: stress relief, depression, low energy levels and chronic pain.

There are many believers and I am one of them:
life is made easier with the chakras balanced
and fully functioning.

I've just recently learned that our chakras play a huge part in our mental wellbeing. Think how:

every tiny trauma we go through can defines how we live, grow and learn. It is very easy to get stuck there, in the confusion and pain and sadness.

When my chakras are balanced, my body feels lighter and my head is clear. I feel like I've just taken the best nap ever!

#21. Breath, Exercise, Nature. Page 119

Earth cure me. Earth receive my woe.
Rock strengthen me. Rock receive my weakness.
Rain wash my sadness away. Rain receive my doubt.
Sun make sweet my song. Sun receive the anger from my heart.
                    - Nancy Wood. Earth Prayers from Around the World

Breath not only keeps us alive, it is a powerful healing tool. I started taking conscious deep breaths 3-5 times a day when I read that it can help us lose weight! I can't say that has happened but I did notice an increase in patience and energy.

I haven't written about exercise much but there is no doubt that getting the heart rate up at least once a day is good for our mental health. I try not to make it about weight, just overall health. When I have made getting a sweat on a priority, my days are calmer and happier.

Getting outside and fresh air 98.4% of the time activates my creative brain and brings me clarity.

BONUS Mind Tricks

#1. Send Healing to Others.

I started doing this one again during the recent pandemic. It has helped me feel a sense of purpose during the crazy days of Covid-19.

- Lay down and close your eyes

- Visualize grabbing all the pain, uncertainty and ugly sickness from you, those in your house and then expand to homes around you, the entire neighbourhood.

- Visualize grabbing all of the pain, frustration, disease and drag it to a huge spinning cloud (think 1970s Spiderman cartoon here).

- Expand the collection of pain and suffering as far as you want. The whole town, city, province/state, country. Even the WHOLE WIDE WORLD.

- Gather is all, spin in the cloud and blow it out to the sky with deep breaths.

- With a huge deep breath, blow the entire bundle as far out as you can imagine. Watch it explode and disintegrate far away from all of us. Never to return.

#2. Body smiles.

If you have read Elizabeth Gilbert's book or have watched the movie, you will recognize this one. In Elizabeth's memoir, her spiritual teacher in Bali encourages her to lighten up a bit by smiling with her liver while meditating. He says: "Why do they always look so serious in Yoga? You make a serious face like this, you scare away good energy. To meditate, only you must smile. Smile with face, smile with mind, and good energy will come to you and clean away dirty energy. Even smile in your liver. Practice tonight at the hotel. Not to hurry, not to try too hard. Too serious, you make you sick. You can call good energy with a smile."

He guides her through the following technique. Similar to FAB #9 Zip, I find doing this in the morning is the best because it is an awesome excuse to stay a bit longer.

- Start at your toes and work your way through your whole body. I really don't follow any rules here.

- If I have time, I focus on each and every toe and as many body parts as I can think of.

- With continual deep breaths (I focus on healing breath reaching the body part I'm focusing on and breathing out the bad, ugly, negative).

- Thank your body for all it does for you every minute of every day.

- I imagine every part that I am focusing on to be healthy, happy and smiling. I would at least do one full, deep breath per body part but more is a-ok!

Try to do the same for five minutes every day for at least 21 days.

#3. Music (and Sing and Dance!).

Play it (few of my favs are: Love Pink's 'Perfect', Ben Folds Five 'Always Someone Cooler than You', anything Air Supply) inside, in the car or the best for me is listening while I go for a walk. Sing and dance to it. Have a playlist of songs that make you feel awesome when you are feeling gross, uninspired, sad, regret, sorry for yourself, dwelling on the past ...

#4. No Rules!!

Within reason of course. We are constantly bombarded with information from our computers, phones, TVs, printed materials telling us how we 'should' live and feel. We are getting advice from all over the world. I think it is important to not put too much pressure on ourselves especially when we are feeling stressed, overwhelmed and close to breaking point. My 40th birthday month I tried, "No Rules!" month. I didn't floss or even brush my teeth sometimes. I ate the last piece of pizza and binge watch shows without feeling guilty. I let myself slack on dinner prep, or even change out of my clothes to go to bed! I took the lead from how I was feeling everyday when I woke up and proceeded without the 'shoulds'.

Mental Wellness

T	P	R	R	S	E	L	M	T	R	U	S	T	P
N	E	E	K	R	F	S	U	G	T	E	M	P	U
E	E	E	I	E	R	M	I	F	R	T	D	I	Y
M	L	T	N	K	L	E	G	G	E	E	I	Z	K
A	S	N	D	N	U	E	W	N	C	T	B	C	I
R	O	U	N	O	E	W	S	I	M	B	A	O	E
E	L	L	E	B	L	G	S	L	R	K	P	R	S
P	U	O	S	U	S	I	O	A	H	E	E	T	G
M	T	V	S	L	V	U	T	E	H	U	M	O	R
E	I	Y	T	E	M	B	O	H	L	H	F	H	P
T	O	N	E	P	N	F	A	B	U	L	O	U	S
O	N	D	N	I	M	Y	H	T	L	A	E	H	T
T	S	M	R	A	L	Y	P	A	R	E	H	T	H
P	E	R	I	P	A	T	I	E	N	T	N	E	E

SOLUTIONS
TEMPERAMENT
HEALING
VOLUNTEER
GRATEFUL
DECISIVE
PATIENT
THERAPY
FABULOUS
KINDNESS
EGO
HEALTHYMIND
REWIRE
SOBER
BONKERS
HUMOR
TRUST
ZIP
SLEEP

Play this puzzle online at : https://thewordsearch.com/puzzle/1145368/

Get Carey's help with putting your FAB Mind Tricks into action at
careywilkinsonlee.com!